Early Praise for *Deploying JRuby*

Deploying with JRuby is the definitive text on getting JRuby applications up and running. Joe has pulled together a great collection of deployment knowledge, and the JRuby story is much stronger as a result.

➤ **Charles Oliver Nutter**
   JRuby Core team member and coauthor, *Using JRuby*

Deploying with JRuby answers all of the most frequently asked questions regarding real-world use of JRuby that I have seen, including many we were not able to answer in *Using JRuby*. Whether you're coming to JRuby from Ruby or Java, Joe fills in all the gaps you'll need to deploy JRuby with confidence.

➤ **Nick Sieger**
   JRuby Core team member and coauthor, *Using JRuby*

This book is an excellent guide to navigating the various JRuby deployment options. Joe is fair in his assessment of these technologies and describes a clear path for getting your Ruby application up and running on the JVM.

➤ **Bob McWhirter**
   TorqueBox team lead at Red Hat

Essential reading to learn not only how to deploy web applications on JRuby but also why.

➤ **David Calavera**
   Creator of Trinidad

Deploying with JRuby

Deliver Scalable Web Apps Using the JVM

Joe Kutner

The Pragmatic Bookshelf

Dallas, Texas • Raleigh, North Carolina

Our Pragmatic courses, workshops, and other products can help you and your team create better software and have more fun. For more information, as well as the latest Pragmatic titles, please visit us at *http://pragprog.com*.

The team that produced this book includes:

Brian P. Hogan (editor)
Potomac Indexing, LLC (indexer)
Kim Wimpsett (copyeditor)
David J Kelly (typesetter)
Janet Furlow (producer)
Juliet Benda (rights)
Ellie Callahan (support)

Printed in the United States of America.
ISBN-13: 978-1-934356-97-5
Printed on acid-free paper.
Book version: P1.0—July 2012

Contents

Acknowledgments

It's a remarkable feeling to have other people offer their time and energy to help improve a project that is your own creation. I have been fortunate enough to experience this feeling multiple times over the course of writing this book, so it is important that I try to thank the people who helped make it possible.

I must first thank the reviewers of my book who do not know me. I was shocked by the attention to detail and wise feedback they provided in making my book a finished product. Thank you to Jeff Holland, Matt Margolis, Stephen Wolff, Sam Rose, Tibor Simic, Frederico Tomassetti, Charley Stran, Ian Dees, Kevin Gisi, Wil Moore III, and the dozens of people who reported errata while this book was in beta. I consider you all to be my friends!

Thank you to my wonderful colleagues for their experience, wisdom, and editorial feedback as I worked on this project. They helped me in both the proposal process and the review process: Lyle Johnson, Matt Blackmon, Joshua Rufer, Bryan Powell, Bret Young, Matt Smith, and Robert Miller. This paragraph does not do our friendship justice. Thank you.

I would also like to thank the staff at the Pragmatic Bookshelf: Susannah Pfalzer, Dave Thomas, Andy Hunt, and probably a whole bunch of other people I don't know about. Above all, thank you to Brian P. Hogan, my editor. You have been fair and kind in dealing with much of the crude prose I've thrown your way. Thank you for helping me with this book and to become a better writer.

It is also important that I thank the creators of the technologies I have written about. This book would not have been possible without their hard work. Thank you to Charles Nutter, Thomas Enebo, Nick Seiger, and the rest of the JRuby team. You are the most amazing group in all of the open source world. Thank you to David Calavera and Karol Bucek of the Trinidad project. Even during the holiday season, these brilliant programmers made themselves available to answer my questions. Thank you to Ben Browning, Toby Crawley, Bob McWhirter, Lance Ball, Jim Crossley, Marek Goldmann, and the rest of the TorqueBox team. Of this group, I must especially thank Ben and Toby, who also provided me with extremely insightful reviews. I hope that I have done justice to the effort these people have put into the technologies covered by this book. I owe them all my deepest gratitude and a free beverage.

Finally, I would like to thank my wife and son. I could not have completed this project without your love and support.

Preface

Your website has just crashed, and you're losing money. The application is built on Rails, runs on MRI, and is served up with Mongrel and Apache. Having this kind of infrastructure means that you're managing more processes than you can count on two hands.

The background jobs are run with Resque,[1] the scheduled jobs are run with cron, and the long-running jobs use Ruby daemons,[2] which are monitored by monit.[3] It's going to take some time to figure out which component is the culprit because you have no centralized management interface. Standing up a new server will take almost as long because the infrastructure is so complex. But the website has to get back online if you are going to stay in business.

The problem I've just described is all too common. It has happened to everyone from small start-ups to large companies that use Rails to serve millions of requests. Their infrastructure is complex, and the myriad components are difficult to manage because they are heterogeneous and decentralized in nature. Even worse, Rubyists have become comfortable with this way of doing things, and many think it is the only way of doing things. But that is not the case.

The recent growth and increased adoption of the Java Virtual Machine (JVM) as a platform for Ruby applications has opened many new doors. Deployment strategies that were not possible with MRI Ruby are now an option because of the JVM's built-in management tools and support for native operating system threads. Ruby programmers can leverage these features by deploying their applications on JRuby.

It's common for Ruby programmers to think that JRuby deployment will look identical to deployment with MRI Ruby (that is, running lots of JVM processes

---

1. https://github.com/defunkt/resque
2. http://daemons.rubyforge.org/
3. http://mmonit.com/monit/

behind a load balancer and putting any asynchronous background jobs in a separate process). On the other hand, Java programmers tend to deploy JRuby applications the same way they deploy Java applications. This often requires lots of XML and custom build configurations, which negate many of the benefits of a more dynamic language such as Ruby. But there are much better options than both Ruby and Java programmers are used to.

In this book, we'll explore the most popular and well-supported methods for deploying JRuby. There is a surprising amount of flexibility in the processes and platforms that can be used, which allows Ruby and Java programmers to tailor their deployments to suit many different environments.

What's in This Book?

Over the course of this book, we're going to rescue the application that was described at the beginning of the chapter. We'll do this by porting it to JRuby and deploying it in a way that will simplify its infrastructure and improve its ability to scale.

The application's name is Twitalytics, and it's a powerful Twitter client. (As you probably know, Twitter is a social networking website that's used to post short status updates, called *tweets*.) Twitalytics tracks public tweets about an organization and performs analytic computations against data captured in those tweets in order to discover trends and make predictions. But it can't handle its current load.

Twitalytics has several background jobs that are used to stream tweets into the application, perform analytics, and clean up the database as it grows. In addition, it receives a large volume of HTTP requests for traditional web traffic. But doing this on MRI means running everything in separate processes, which consumes more resources than our systems can handle.

We'll begin rescuing Twitalytics in Chapter 1, *Getting Started with JRuby*, on page 1. We'll discuss what makes JRuby a better deployment platform and why we want to use it for our application. Then we'll port Twitalytics to JRuby and package it into an archive file with the Warbler gem. But before we can deploy it, we'll need to create an environment where it can run.

In Chapter 2, *Creating a Deployment Environment*, on page 19, we'll set up a virtual production server that will simulate a real deployment target. We'll provision it with the essential components of any production JRuby environment, which means these steps will apply not only to Twitalytics but to any JRuby deployment. You'll also learn how to automate this process to make it more reliable. We'll create a new server for each deployment strategy we use in this book, and the automated scripts will save us from having to re-create this environment each time.

Once we've completed the setup of our production server, we'll be ready to deploy. In Chapter 3, *Deploying an Archive File*, on page 37, we'll write a script that deploys the archive file we created earlier. You'll learn how this process differs from the more common practice of deploying a Ruby application as a directory of loose files. The script we'll write will be more portable than tools like Capistrano. We'll also deploy Twitalytics to the cloud with the CloudBees platform.

The Warbler gem gives us a quick way to get started with JRuby. But it's just a stepping stone on our path to better performance. As the book progresses, we'll improve our deployment by running Twitalytics on some JRuby web servers.

The next two chapters of the book will be dedicated to the lightweight Trinidad web server. Trinidad lets us deploy applications much like we would with MRI-based Rails applications using tools like Capistrano. But we'll find that JRuby allows us to reduce the complexity of this kind of deployment environment while increasing its reliability and portability. In Chapter 4, *Creating a Trinidad Application*, on page 57, we'll port not only the part of Twitalytics that handles web requests but also its background jobs to Trinidad. Then we'll set up our virtual server and deploy our application in Chapter 5, *Deploying a Trinidad Application*, on page 75. The resulting architecture will be friendly and familiar to Rubyists.

But we still won't be making the most of what the JVM has to offer. To do that, we'll need a new kind of container.

In Chapter 6, *Creating a TorqueBox Application*, on page 103, we'll introduce the concept of an application server. This kind of deployment is unique when compared to traditional Ruby deployments because it provides a complete environment to run any kind of program, not just a web application. We'll show how this eliminates the need for external processes and provides a centralized management interface. In Chapter 7, *Deploying a TorqueBox Application*, on page 133, we'll push to a production server running TorqueBox. But ultimately, we'll deploy our application to a TorqueBox cluster in Chapter 8, *Clustering a TorqueBox Application*, on page 149. This will give us the most advanced deployment environment available to any Ruby application.

An overview of each strategy covered in this book is listed in the following table:

	Warbler	Trinidad	TorqueBox
Built-in web server	Winstone	Apache Tomcat	JBoss AS
Archive file deployment	WAR file	WAR file	Knob file
Capistrano deployment	No	Yes	Yes
Background jobs	No	Yes	Yes
Clustering support	No	No	Yes

Deciding on the right platform for each application is a function of these attributes. But getting an application up and running on one of these platforms is just part of the job. We also need to keep it running. To do that, we'll use some built-in JVM tools to inspect our new platform.

Chapter 9, *Managing a JRuby Deployment*, on page 163 will present some tools for monitoring, managing, and configuring a deployed JRuby application. These tools are independent of any deployment strategy and can be used to monitor the memory consumption, performance, and uptime of any Java process. Finally, Chapter 10, *Using a Continuous Integration Server*, on page 181 will introduce a tool for producing reliable and consistent deployments.

Twitalytics is a Rails application, and we'll use this to our advantage as we deploy it. But all of the server technologies we'll use work equally well with any Rack-compliant framework (such as Sinatra[4] or Merb[5]). In fact, the steps we'll use to package and deploy Twitalytics would be identical for these other frameworks. Warbler, Trinidad, and TorqueBox provide a few hooks that make deploying a Rails application more concise in some cases (such as automatically packaging bundled gems). But the workflow is the same.

When you encounter Rails-specific features in this book, be aware that this is only for demonstration purposes and not because the frameworks are pigeonholed to work with Rails. In fact, Rails works with these servers because it is Rack-based.

Who Is This Book For?

This book is for programmers, system administrators, and DevOps[6] professionals who want to use JRuby to power their applications but are not familiar with how this new platform will change their infrastructure.

---

4. http://www.sinatrarb.com/
5. http://www.merbivore.com/
6. http://en.wikipedia.org/wiki/DevOps

It is not required that you have any experience with JRuby. This book is written from the perspective of someone who is familiar with MRI-based Ruby deployments but wants a modern deployment strategy for their applications. Some of the concepts we'll discuss may be more familiar to programmers with Java backgrounds, but it is not required that you have any experience with Java or its associated technologies.

The No-Java-Code Promise

You will not have to write any Java code as you work your way through this book. That's not what this book is about. It is about deploying Ruby applications on the JVM. The technologies and tools that you will be introduced to in this book hide the XML and Java code from you. As the TorqueBox developers like to say, "[They] write Java so you don't have to."[7]

You may want to include some Java code in your application. Or you may want to make calls to some Java libraries. That is entirely your choice. If you want to write your programs exclusively in Ruby and deploy them on the Java Virtual Machine—like so many of us do—then go ahead.

There are many reasons to deploy Ruby applications on the JVM, and using Java libraries and APIs is just one of them. In this book, you'll learn how to get the most out of the JVM without writing any Java code.

Conventions

The examples in this book can be run on Linux, Mac, Windows, and many other operating systems. But some small changes to the command-line statements may be required for certain platforms.

We'll be using notation from bash, the default shell on Mac OS X and many Linux distributions, so the $ prompt will be used for all command-line examples. Windows command prompts typically use something like C:\> instead, so when you see a command like this:

```
$ bundle install
```

you'll know not to type the dollar sign and to read it like this:

```
C:\> bundle install
```

The commands we'll use are mostly compatible between Windows and bash systems (such as cd and mkdir). In the cases where they are not compatible,

---

7.   http://vimeo.com/27494052

the appropriate commands for both systems will be spelled out. One in particular is the rm command, which will look like this:

```
$ rm temp.txt
$ rm -rf tmp/
```

On Windows this should be translated to these two commands, respectively:

```
C:\> del temp.txt
C:\> rd /s /q tmp/
```

Another Unix notation that is used in this book is the ~ (tilde) to represent a user's home directory. When you see a command like this:

```
$ cd ~/code/twitalytics
```

you can translate it to Windows 7 as this command:

```
C:\> cd C:\Users\yourname\code\twitalytics
```

On earlier versions of Windows, the user's home directory can be found in the Documents and Settings directory. You can also use the %USERPROFILE% environment variable. Its value is the location of the current user's profile directory.

Other than these minor notation changes, the examples in this book are compatible with Windows by virtue of the Java Virtual Machine.

Preparing Your Environment

Four software packages are required to run the examples in the book. They are listed here along with the version that is needed:

- Java Development Kit (JDK) 6 (aka 1.6)
- JRuby 1.6.7
- Git 1.7
- Bundler 1.0

Java 7 was released in July 2011 and is supported by JRuby 1.6.7, but this newer version of the JVM is not readily available on all operating systems. To ensure the consistency of the steps in this book, we will use Java 6. However, you are encouraged to try Java 7 if your platform supports it.[8]

Java is supported in one form or another on a wide range of operating systems including Linux, Mac, Windows, and more, but the installation process will be different for each.

---

8.   http://www.engineyard.com/blog/2011/getting-started-with-jruby-and-java-7/

Installing Java

On Debian-based Linux platforms, such as Ubuntu, the JVM can be installed with APT, like this:

```
$ sudo apt-get install openjdk-6-jdk
```

On Fedora, Oracle Linux, and Red Hat, the JVM can be install with the yum command, like this:

```
$ su -c "yum install java-1.6.0-openjdk"
```

For Mac OS X systems, Apple provides a JDK version 6, and versions of Mac OS X prior to 10.7 (Lion) ship with the JDK. If you are running Lion, you can install the JDK by opening the Java Preferences application under the /Applications/Utilities/ directory. The first time this program is opened, we'll see a dialog like the one in Figure 1, *Mac OS X prompt to install Java,* on page xviii. Follow its instructions to install the Java runtime. If the dialog does not appear, then the JDK is already installed.

For Windows systems, we'll need to use the Oracle JDK. Download and run the binary installer from the Oracle website.[9] After the installation completes, we'll need to set the JAVA_HOME variable. (The exact path may vary).

```
C:\> SET JAVA_HOME="C:\Program Files\Java\jdk1.6.0_27"
```

In all cases, we can check that the JVM was installed correctly by running this command:

```
$ java -version
java version "1.6.0_07"
Java(TM) SE Runtime Environment (build 1.6.0_07-b06-153)
Java HotSpot(TM) 64-Bit Server VM (build 1.6.0_07-b06-57, mixed mode)
```

Now that the JVM is ready, we can put JRuby on our machine.

Installing JRuby

The preferred method for installing JRuby on Unix and Linux systems requires the Ruby Version Manager (RVM). It's preferred not only because it makes JRuby easy to install but also because it treats JRuby just like any other Ruby platform. This allows us to use the ruby and gem commands without putting the j character in front of them or prefixing every other command with the jruby -S command. RVM is compatible only with bash systems, which does not include Windows. Installing JRuby on Windows will be described in a moment, but if you are using a bash system, run this command to install RVM:

---

9.   http://www.oracle.com/technetwork/java/javase/downloads/index.html

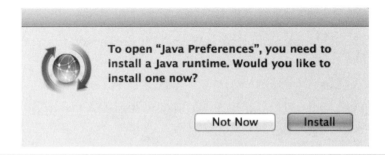

Figure 1—Mac OS X prompt to install Java

```
$ bash < <( curl http://rvm.beginrescueend.com/releases/rvm-install-head )
```

You'll also have to reload your shell. The most dependable way to do this is to close the current terminal and open a new one. Now we can use RVM to install JRuby with this command:

```
$ rvm install jruby
jruby-1.6.7 - #fetching
jruby-1.6.7 - #extracted to ~/.rvm/src/jruby-1.6.7 (already extracted)
Building Nailgun
jruby-1.6.7 - #installing to ~/.rvm/rubies/jruby-1.6.7
jruby-1.6.7 - #importing default gemsets (/home/vagrant/.rvm/gemsets/)
Copying across included gems
Building native extensions. This could take a while...
Successfully installed jruby-launcher-1.0.12-java
1 gem installed
```

We'll also need to set JRuby as the default Ruby.

```
$ rvm --default use jruby
Using ~/.rvm/gems/jruby-1.6.7
```

If you are using a system that does not support RVM, such as Windows, then JRuby can be installed manually with these three steps:

1. Download the JRuby binaries from the official website.[10]
2. Unpack the downloaded file, which will create a jruby-<version> directory.
3. Add jruby-<version>/bin to the PATH.

Without RVM, we'll have to modify the commands that are used in this book. RVM allows us to invoke JRuby without using the jruby or jgem command, so we'll have to change all ruby commands in this book to jruby commands. We'll also need to prefix any other commands (such as bundle, gem, and rails) with the jruby -S prefix, like this:

---

10. http://jruby.org/download

```
$ jruby -S bundle install
```

We can check that JRuby was installed correctly with this command:

```
$ ruby -v
jruby 1.6.7 (ruby-1.8.7p357) (2012-02-22 3e82bc8) ...
```

You will *never* be asked to run any of the examples in this book with MRI Ruby, so remember that when you see the ruby, gem, rake, or similar commands, you are expected to be running them with JRuby.

Next, we need to install Git.

Installing Git

Git is a source control management tool that allows us to track versions of our code. We'll be using Git to switch between different versions of Twitalytics as we deploy it to new platforms. Follow the instructions for downloading and installing Git from the official website.[11]

It's OK to use some other form of version control if you'd prefer, but the examples in this book will be specific to Git. The examples will even work without version control software, but that is not recommended. The source code for each branch we'll create is available from http://pragprog.com/titles/jkdepj/source_code, so instead of switching branches, you can change to the directory that corresponds to the chapter you're reading.

Getting the Source Code

Now we're ready to set up the Twitalytics application. We'll start by downloading the source code from http://pragprog.com/titles/jkdepj/source_code. Unpack the downloaded file and put it in your home directory. This will create a code directory and inside of that will be a twitalytics directory, which contains the baseline code for the application (in other words, the MRI-based code).

We need to change directories into this location and initialize it as a Git repository.

```
$ cd twitalytics
$ git init
$ git add .
$ git commit -m "initial commit"
```

Next, we need to install Bundler, a dependency management tool for Ruby, by running the following command:

---

11. http://git-scm.com/download

```
$ gem install bundler
```

Now we can use Bundler to install Twitalytics' dependencies by running this command:

```
$ bundle install --without production
```

We've added the --without production option to exclude the pg gem, which requires that PostgreSQL be installed. We'll take care of this later in the book by switching to some JRuby database adapters that are just as fast and don't rely on native code.

Our development environment is ready, but we won't be able to run Twitalytics with JRuby yet; it works only under MRI. We'll port it to JRuby in Chapter 1, *Getting Started with JRuby*, on page 1.

Online Resources

Several online resources can help if you're having trouble setting up your environment or running any of the examples in this book.

For Java-related problems, the Java.net community has forums[12] and numerous Java-related articles.

For JRuby-related problems, the official JRuby website[13] has links to several community outlets. The most useful of these are the mailing list[14] and the #jruby IRC channel on FreeNode.[15]

For Trinidad-related problems, there is a mailing list[16] and a wiki.[17]

For TorqueBox-related problems, there is a mailing list,[18] extensive documentation,[19] and the #torquebox IRC channel on FreeNode.

---

12. http://www.java.net/forum
13. http://jruby.org/community
14. http://xircles.codehaus.org/projects/jruby/lists
15. http://freenode.net/
16. http://groups.google.com/group/rails-trinidad
17. https://github.com/trinidad/trinidad/wiki
18. http://torquebox.org/community/mailing_lists/
19. http://torquebox.org/documentation/

CHAPTER 1

Getting Started with JRuby

JRuby is a high-performance platform that can scale to meet demand without the headaches of an MRI-based deployment. Those headaches are often the result of running a dozen or more processes on a single server that all need to be monitored, balanced, and occasionally restarted. JRuby avoids these problems by simplifying the architecture that's required to run an application. In this chapter, we're going to port our application to JRuby so that we can take advantage of this simplicity and the scalability that results from it. But in order to run the application in production, we'll need a way to deploy it. For this, we'll use Warbler.[1]

Warbler is a gem that can package our source code into an archive file that we can deploy without the need for tools like Capistrano. This makes the process more flexible, portable, and faster.

We'll be able to get started with Warbler quickly, but we'll eventually outgrow it. Warbler is primarily a tool for deploying the part of an application that handles web requests, so it won't help us with things like background jobs. It also makes it difficult to run the same web server we use in production on our development machines. But it's the quickest way to get an application running on JRuby, and that's why we'll use Warbler as our first step to saving Twitalytics.

In *Preface*, on page xi, you were introduced to Twitalytics, which needs help. Its infrastructure is too complex, and it can't handle the volume of requests the site is receiving. We don't have time to port the daemons and background jobs to a new framework, but we need to get the part of the application that handles HTTP requests deployed on JRuby. If we can do that, we'll be able to handle lots of concurrent requests without hogging our system's memory.

---

1. https://github.com/jruby/warbler

These time constraints make Warbler a great solution. It won't maximize our use of the JVM, but it will allow us to take advantage of the most important parts. We'll be able to service all of our site's web requests from a single process without changing much of our code. The drawback is that we will have to make changes to our deployment process, so there is much to learn. Let's begin by discussing why we want to use JRuby in the first place.

1.1 What Makes JRuby So Great?

A production JRuby environment has fewer moving parts than traditional Ruby environments. This is possible because of the JVM's support for native operating system threads. Instead of managing dozens of processes, JRuby can use multiple threads of execution to do work in parallel. MRI has threads, but only one thread can execute Ruby code at a time. This has led to some complex workarounds to achieve concurrency.

Deployment with MRI usually requires a type of architecture that handles HTTP requests by placing either Apache[2] or a similar web server in front of a pool of application instances that run in separate processes. An example of this using Mongrel is illustrated in Figure 2, *Traditional MRI web application architecture*, on page 3. There are many problems with this kind of architecture, and those problems have been realized by Twitter, GitHub, and countless others. They include the following:

Stuck processes
Sometimes the processes will get into a stuck state and need to be killed by an external tool like god or monit.

Slow restarts
There is a lot of overhead in starting a new process. Several instances may end up fighting each other for resources if they are restarted at the same time.

Memory growth
Each of the processes keeps its own copy of an application, along with Rails and any supporting gems, in memory. Each new instance means we'll also need more memory for the server.

Several frameworks, such as Unicorn, Passenger, and Thin, have been created that try to improve upon this model. But they all suffer from the same underlying constraint. MRI cannot handle multiple requests in the same

---

2.   http://httpd.apache.org/

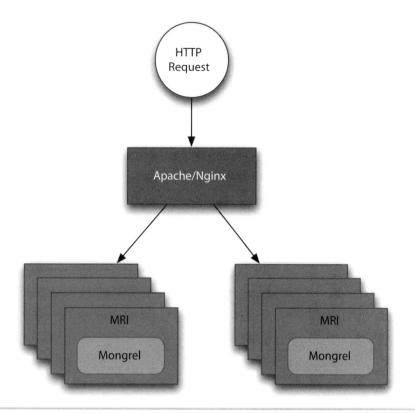

Figure 2— Traditional MRI web application architecture

runtime concurrently. If you want to handle ten requests at the same time, then you need to have ten instances of your application running. No matter how you do it, deploying with MRI means managing lots of processes.

JRuby allows us to use a very similar model but with only one JVM process. Inside this JVM process is a single application instance that handles all of our website's traffic. This works by allowing the platform to create many threads that run against the same application instance in parallel. We can create far more JVM threads than we could MRI processes because they are much lighter weight. This model is illustrated in Figure 3, *Architecture of a JRuby web application*, on page 4, and we can use it to serve many more concurrent requests than an MRI-based system.

We've included Apache in the architecture, but its role on a single instance is greatly reduced. We'll use it to serve up static content and load balance a distributed cluster, but it won't need to distribute requests across multiple processes on a single machine.

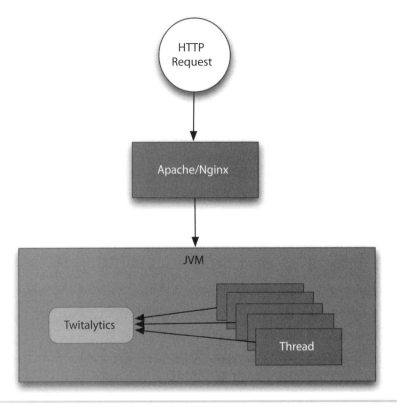

Figure 3—Architecture of a JRuby web application

In the coming chapters, we'll build an architecture like the one we've just described with each of the technologies we use. We'll start with Warbler, which will get us up and running quickly. Let's begin by using Warbler to package a simple Rack application.

1.2 Introducing Warbler

Warbler is a gem that can create a web application archive (WAR) file from a Rails, Merb, or Rack-based application.

A WAR file is a zip file that follows a few conventions, but we don't have to worry about those conventions because Warbler takes care of them for us. What we do need to know is how to use the Warbler commands to package our application.

The WAR file that Warbler creates will be completely self-contained and ready to be deployed to a Java web server. Warbler bundles JRuby, your web

> ### ϟ⁄ Joe asks:
> ## What's in a WAR File?
>
> A WAR file is a special case of Java archive (JAR) file; both are really just zip files. But a WAR file is structured according to a standard that is recognized by all Java web servers. We can take a closer look at this by extracting the WAR file we created in this chapter with any unzipping tool. Inside of it, we find these essential components (among many other things):
>
> ```
> twitalytics.war
> |-- index.html
> |-- META-INF/
>     `-- MANIFEST.MF
> `-- WEB-INF/
>     |-- lib/
>     `-- web.xml
> ```
>
> The top-level directory contains all client-accessible content, which is equivalent to the public directory in a Rails application. This is where we'll find all of the HTML files, images, and other static content. The WEB-INF directory contains all the dynamic content for our web application. This includes our Ruby scripts, and the Java libraries need to run a JRuby application. The META-INF directory contains basic metadata about the WAR file, such as who created it and when it was created.
>
> Inside the WEB-INF directory is the web.xml file, which is the most important part of the archive. It contains a description of how the components in the web application are put together at runtime. It's similar to the config/application.rb, config/environment.rb, and config/routes.rb files of a Rails application all put together into a single descriptor. Fortunately, Warbler handles the creation of this file for us based on the settings in our config/warbler.rb file.
>
> A WAR file can be digitally signed, which creates a checksum for each file contained in the archive. This is used by a web server to ensure that no one has tampered with it or that it has not been corrupted in some way. If the checksums do not match, then the server won't load the files.

framework, and all of the dependencies needed to adapt a Ruby web application to a Java-based container.

To demonstrate Warbler, let's create the simplest web application we can. First, we'll create a directory called myapp. In that directory, we'll create a config.ru file and put the following code into it:

Warbler/myapp/config.ru
```
run lambda { |env|
    [200, {'Content-Type' => 'text/html'}, 'Hello, World']
}
```

Next, we need to install the Warbler gem to our JRuby gem path with this command:

```
$ gem install warbler
Successfully installed jruby-jars-1.6.7
Successfully installed jruby-rack-1.1.4
Successfully installed rubyzip-0.9.6.1
Successfully installed warbler-1.3.4
4 gems installed
```

Warbler has two JRuby-specific dependencies. The jruby-jars gem includes the core JRuby code and standard library files. This allows other gems to depend on JRuby without freezing to a specific version. The other dependency, the jruby-rack gem, is responsible for adapting the Java web server specification to the Rack specification.

Next, let's use the warble command to create our archive file. In the same directory as the config.ru file we created earlier, we'll run it with the war option.

```
$ warble war
```

This will create a myapp.war file. In Chapter 3, *Deploying an Archive File*, on page 37, we will discuss all the different ways we can deploy this WAR file. For now, we just want to be able to run it so we can demonstrate how Warbler works. To do this, we'll create an executable WAR file. Let's build the WAR file again by running the same command with the executable option.

```
$ warble executable war
```

This will create a WAR file that is capable of running on its own, without the need for a free-standing Java web server. You probably won't want to use this in production, but it will help us test our archive file. We can run it with this command:

```
$ java -jar myapp.war
```

When the server is started, you'll be able to access the application at http://localhost:8080.

That's all you need to know to get started with Warbler. Now let's make some adjustments to the Twitalytics application. It wasn't built to run on JRuby, so it has some code that's specific to MRI. We're going to fix these parts so they work on our new platform.

1.3 Preparing Twitalytics for JRuby

In the previous section, we packaged a simple Rack application that was compatible with JRuby, but Twitalytics is more complex. Before we can package Twitalytics with Warbler, we need to make sure the application is ready for JRuby. In doing so, we'll need to make some changes to our code, so let's branch our Git repository with the following command:

```
$ cd ~/code/twitalytics
$ git checkout -b jruby
Switched to a new branch 'jruby'
```

We'll use this branch to commit our JRuby-specific changes to Twitalytics. But how do we know what changes to make? Fortunately, there is an app that can help us with that. The JRuby-Lint[3] tool can detect most JRuby incompatibilities in an application. It runs through the code base and looks for common gotchas. Let's start by installing the gem.

```
$ gem install jruby-lint
Successfully installed jruby-lint-0.3.1
1 gem installed
```

Next, we'll run the tool from our project's root directory.

```
$ jrlint
JRuby-Lint version 0.3.1
For more on gem compatibility see http://wiki.jruby.org/C-Extension-Alternatives
./Gemfile:19: [gems, warning] Found gem 'therubyracer' which is reported to ...
Try using therubyrhino instead.
./Gemfile:36: [gems, warning] Found gem 'sqlite3' which is reported to have ...
Use activerecord-jdbc-adapter instead along with jdbc-sqlite3.
./app/controllers/company_controller.rb:13: [fork, error] Kernel#fork is not...
Processed 37 files in 1.07 seconds
Found 4 items
```

JRuby-Lint found three problems for us (it says it "Found 4 items" because it will take two changes to fix one of them). The first two problems are the result of gems that are incompatible with JRuby. Our database adapters and therubyracer gem contain native code that cannot run on the JVM. Fixing this will require that we switch to some new libraries. We need to open the Gemfile and look for these lines:

twitalytics/Gemfile
```
platform :ruby do
  gem 'therubyracer'
end
```

---

3. https://github.com/jruby/jruby-lint

This gem provides an embedded JavaScript interpreter for Ruby that uses the V8 engine, which can't run on the JVM. Fortunately, there is an alternative gem called therubyrhino, which embeds a JVM-friendly engine. It's even maintained by the same person.[4] To use it, we need to replace the platform block shown previously with this code:

JRuby/twitalytics/Gemfile
```
platform :jruby do
  gem 'therubyrhino'
end
```

Now we'll run Bundler again (continuing to use the --without production flag that we discussed in *Preface*, on page xi).

```
$ bundle install --without production
```

Our new JavaScript engine has been installed. Next, we'll fix the problem with our database adapters. Look for these lines in the Gemfile:

twitalytics/Gemfile
```
group :production do
  gem 'pg'
end

group :development, :test do
  gem 'sqlite3'
end
```

Database adapters also use a lot of native code that doesn't work with JRuby. Because of this, JRuby provides a set of replacement adapters that are built upon the extremely mature, secure, and robust Java Database Connectivity (JDBC) libraries. Let's replace the earlier groups with this code:

JRuby/twitalytics/Gemfile
```
gem 'activerecord-jdbc-adapter', :require => false

group :production do
  gem 'jdbc-postgres'
end

group :development, :test do
  gem 'jdbc-sqlite3'
end
```

This will load the ActiveRecord-JDBC adapters for SQLite3 and Postgres, which are JRuby compatible. Furthermore, installing the JDBC adapters won't require the physical database to be present, which means we can

---

4. https://github.com/cowboyd

eliminate the Bundler --without production option that we used earlier. Bundler remembers the --without option, so we need to run the following command to clear the configuration:

```
$ bundle install --without none
```

The *none* group is a dummy that clears our previous configuration. Subsequent runs of Bundler won't require any flags.

Now let's give the new adapter a simple test by running our migrations.

```
$ rake db:migrate
JRuby limited openssl loaded. http://jruby.org/openssl
gem install jruby-openssl for full support.
==  CreateStatuses: migrating =================================================
-- create_table(:statuses)
   -> 0.0050s
   -> 0 rows
==  CreateStatuses: migrated (0.0050s) ========================================

==  CreateAnalytics: migrating ================================================
-- create_table(:analytics)
   -> 0.0030s
   -> 1 rows
==  CreateAnalytics: migrated (0.0040s) =======================================
```

Our database configuration and local databases are ready. Let's run jrlint again and see how we are doing.

```
$ jrlint
JRuby-Lint version 0.3.1
./app/controllers/company_controller.rb:13: [fork, error] Kernel#fork is not ...
Processed 38 files in 1.07 seconds
Found 1 items
```

Uh-oh, Twitalytics is using the Kernel#fork() method, which is not supported on JRuby. Let's open the app/controllers/company_controller.rb file and take a look.

twitalytics/app/controllers/company_controller.rb
```
def update
  child = fork do
    post_update(params[:status_text])
  end
  Process.detach(child)

  flash[:notice] = "Status updated!"
  redirect_to company_path
end

private
```

```
def post_update(text)
  # We won't actually update because that requires an OAuth token.
  # Twitter.update(text)
  sleep 10
  puts "update posted successfully"
end
```

It appears that sending the status update to Twitter was often hanging or taking too long. This caused our users to wait excessively for the browser to respond. After a few seconds, they probably just closed the window. We don't want our customers to leave the Twitalytics site, so it's important that the Twitter updates happen in the background.

Using Kernel#fork() isn't the healthiest way to fire and forget a process. If things don't go right, the child process can become a zombie. Too many zombies can eventually bring down our system. Furthermore, there is no constraint around how many child processes the application can spawn. A denial-of-service attack or even an innocent heavy load could easily flood our OS with processes.

It would be wise to fix this problem regardless of porting to JRuby. Fortunately, with JRuby we can still achieve the parallelism that Kernel#fork() gave us without pushing the job to Resque or some other message queue.

We could replace the call to Kernel#fork() with a call to Thread.new(). That would make the code compatible with JRuby and allow it to run in parallel. But it would not prevent an unbounded number of threads from being created in the same way that forking allowed an unbounded number of processes to be created.

A better solution uses a thread pool. Fortunately, several libraries can make this easy for us. We'll use get_back,[5] a Ruby gem for making any method run asynchronously. Add the following code to the :jruby platform block in our Gemfile and run bundle install:

JRuby/twitalytics/Gemfile
```
gem 'get_back'
```

Now we can declaratively make the post_udpate(text) method run from a thread pool. First, we'll modify the CompanyController so that it extends the GetBack::JoJo module.

JRuby/twitalytics/app/controllers/company_controller.rb
```
class CompanyController < ApplicationController
  include TwitterUtil
  extend GetBack::JoJo
```

---

5.   https://github.com/jkutner/get_back

Then, we'll remove the call to the Kernel#fork() and tell the post_update(text) method to get back.

```
JRuby/twitalytics/app/controllers/company_controller.rb
def update
  post_update(params[:status_text])
  flash[:notice] = "Status updated!"
  redirect_to company_path
end

private

def post_update(text)
  # We won't actually update because that requires an OAuth token.
  # Twitter.update(text)
  sleep 10
  puts "update posted successfully"
end

get_back :post_update, :pool => 10
```

The :pool option creates a fixed-size thread pool with ten threads, which means that only ten updates can be posted simultaneously. If an eleventh post comes along and the ten threads are still busy, it will wait until one becomes available.

The get_back gem is ideal for simple tasks such as posting a Twitter status. But if your application does a lot of background processing, you'll probably benefit from a platform that provides features such as durability, monitoring, and clustering. We'll introduce one like this in Chapter 6, *Creating a TorqueBox Application*, on page 103.

The status update doesn't require advanced monitoring, so we've fixed the forking problem. Let's run jrlint one last time to make sure everything is OK.

```
$ jrlint
JRuby-Lint version 0.3.0
Processed 34 files in 2.84 seconds
OK
```

Now let's make sure everything is working by migrating our test database and running our unit tests (note that you may need to prefix the rspec command with bundle exec depending on your system configuration).

```
$ RAILS_ENV=test rake db:migrate
...
$ rspec spec/
JRuby limited openssl loaded. http://jruby.org/openssl
gem install jruby-openssl for full support.
```

```
FF.....

Failures:

...

Finished in 0.551 seconds
7 examples, 2 failures

Failed examples:

rspec ./spec/controllers/company_controller_spec.rb:6 # CompanyController GET ...
rspec ./spec/controllers/customers_controller_spec.rb:6 # CustomersController ...
```

Oops, we have a couple failures. As you can see from the first line in the RSpec output, we have limited support for OpenSSL. Ruby OpenSSL is a native library, which JRuby can't use. Fortunately, JRuby alerts us to this as soon as the runtime starts and suggests that we install the jruby-openssl gem. Let's do that by adding the following line to the platform :jruby block of our Gemfile and running bundle install:

JRuby/twitalytics/Gemfile
```
gem 'jruby-openssl'
```

Now we can run the tests again and see whether that fixed the problem.

```
$ rspec spec/
.......

Finished in 4.02 seconds
7 examples, 0 failures
```

Excellent. Let's boot the application with WEBrick.

```
$ rails server
=> Booting WEBrick
=> Rails 3.2.1 application starting in development on http://0.0.0.0:3000
=> Call with -d to detach
=> Ctrl-C to shutdown server
[2011-10-21 15:56:25] INFO WEBrick 1.3.1
[2011-10-21 15:56:25] INFO ruby 1.8.7 (2011-08-23) [java]
[2011-10-21 15:56:25] INFO WEBrick::HTTPServer#start: pid=9083 port=3000
```

Now browse to http://localhost:3000, and you'll see the page pictured in Figure 4, *The Twitalytics dashboard*, on page 13.

Let's follow the Company link so we can test the changes we made to the update() action. It will open a page with our account's updates and a text box for posting a status, as pictured in Figure 5, *The Twitalytics status update page*, on page 14. Fill the text box with something and click the Post button

Figure 4—The Twitalytics dashboard

(don't worry, it won't actually post). The browser will return immediately, and ten seconds later you'll see this line in your log file:

```
update posted successfully
```

Congratulations. You ported an application to JRuby. Before we move on, let's commit our changes to the Git repository with the following commands:

```
$ git add .
$ git commit -m "Ported to JRuby"
```

Now we're ready to package it with Warbler.

1.4   Configuring Warbler for Twitalytics

OK, we don't have to configure Warbler for production. It knows Twitalytics is a Rails application and will package it with a nice set of defaults, but we are going to elect to make a few small configuration changes. Before we do, let's branch our Git repository again.

```
$ git checkout -b warbler
Switched to a new branch 'warbler'
```

Now we can safely configure Warbler while preserving our jruby branch.

Warbler does not package a Rails application's db directory into the WAR file by default. But we need to tell Warbler to include it because the path to our development SQLite database in config/database.yml is relative. First, we'll create a config/warble.rb file by running this command:

```
$ warble config
```

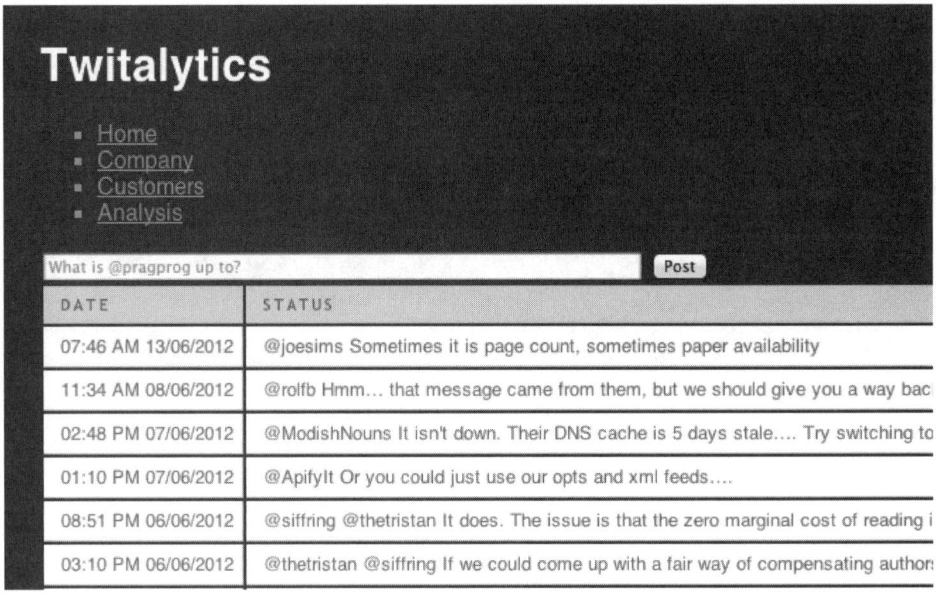

Figure 5—The Twitalytics status update page

Now let's edit the new file. It contains a wealth of instructions and examples for the different configuration options, which are helpful to read. You never know what you might need to change. Don't worry about preserving its contents. You can always re-create it by running warble config again. Given that safety net, let's replace the contents of config/warble.rb file with this code:

```
Warbler/twitalytics/config/warble.rb
Warbler::Config.new do |config|
  config.jar_name = "twitalytics"
  config.dirs << "db"
  config.excludes = FileList["**/*/*.box"]
  config.bundle_without = []
end
```

The configuration shown previously sets the name that will be used for the archive file to *twitalytics*, which ensures it's the same in every environment (the default value is the name of the root directory). Then it adds the db directory to our package. We need to do this only because we're using a SQLite database. As a side effect, we'll have an easy way to run our database migrations against the PostgreSQL database on the production server.

We've cleared the bundle_without list because the defaults exclude *development* and *test* from our WAR file. But we'll need these to test our WAR and also run some Rake tasks later. We've also excluded all .box files, which you'll learn about in Chapter 2, *Creating a Deployment Environment*, on page 19.

Let's test it by creating our first Twitalytics WAR file.

```
$ warble executable war
Creating twitalytics.war
```

Great! Now let's run it. The WAR file executes in production mode by default, so we'll have to be explicit about our RAILS_ENV.

```
$ RAILS_ENV=development java -jar twitalytics.war
[Winstone 2011/10/22 17:37:11] - Beginning extraction from war file
[Winstone 2011/10/22 17:37:13] - WARNING: The Servlet 2.4/2.5 spec XSD was ...
[Winstone 2011/10/22 17:37:13] - No webapp classes folder found - /private/...
[webapp 2011/10/22 17:37:13] - Warning: no max runtimes specified.
[webapp 2011/10/22 17:37:13] - jruby 1.6.7 (ruby-1.8.7-p357) (2012-02-22 3e...
[webapp 2011/10/22 17:37:13] - Info: using runtime pool timeout of 30 seconds
[webapp 2011/10/22 17:37:13] - Warning: no min runtimes specified.
[webapp 2011/10/22 17:37:13] - Warning: no max runtimes specified.
[Winstone 2011/10/22 17:37:13] - Listener winstone.ajp13.Ajp13Listener not ...
[Winstone 2011/10/22 17:37:13] - Listener winstone.ssl.HttpsListener not fo...
[Winstone 2011/10/22 17:37:13] - Winstone Servlet Engine v0.9.10 running: c...
[Winstone 2011/10/22 17:37:13] - HTTP Listener started: port=8080
```

Now point a browser to http://localhost:8080, and you should see the Twitalytics dashboard again. The first time will take a while to load because Rails has some precompilation to do, but it will warm up after that.

Let's take a closer look at the console output from shortly after we started the WAR file. In particular, take a look at these three lines:

```
[webapp 2011/10/22 17:37:13] - Info: using runtime pool timeout of 30 seconds
[webapp 2011/10/22 17:37:13] - Warning: no min runtimes specified.
[webapp 2011/10/22 17:37:13] - Warning: no max runtimes specified.
```

Warbler is using a pool of application instances to prevent multiple threads from executing against Twitalytics in parallel. This is illustrated in Figure 6, *Architecture of a JRuby runtime pool*, on page 16. The runtime pool is helpful if our application is not thread-safe, but it severely limits the concurrency of our web server. It also requires more memory.

We can configure the size of the runtime pool in the config/warble.rb file. Increasing the maximum number of runtime instances will increase the concurrency of our web server. Reducing the minimum number of instances will improve our server's start-up time. The number of runtimes you should use depends on your server hardware. Each additional runtime will require another in-memory copy of your program. Because each runtime is single-threaded, it's

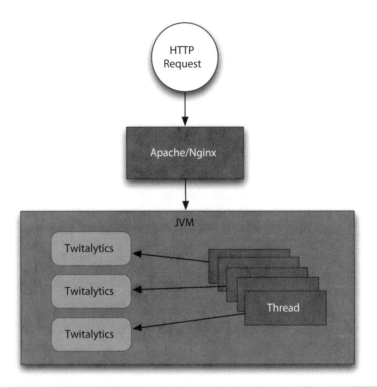

Figure 6— Architecture of a JRuby runtime pool

unlikely that you'll want more instances than you have CPU cores. Let's assume your server hardware has eight cores. A sensible configuration in our config/warbler.rb file might be the following:

```
config.webxml.jruby.min.runtimes = 4
config.webxml.jruby.max.runtimes = 8
```

This is still suboptimal, though. Ideally, we should have one instance of our application in memory with threads running against it in parallel, as illustrated in Figure 3, *Architecture of a JRuby web application*, on page 4. For our application to run correctly in this mode, we have to make sure it is thread-safe.

We can consider our code thread-safe if it behaves correctly when accessed from multiple threads without any synchronization or other coordination on the part of the calling code. That's a mouthful, but thread safety is difficult to define. Formal attempts in academia are complicated and don't provide much practical guidance. Fortunately, there are some good heuristics for making our code thread-safe. The most important is to avoid sharing mutable state between threads. The most common way to accidentally do this in a Ruby program is with class variables.

There is no way to positively ensure that any application is thread-safe. But we've taken a look at Twitalytics' code, so we have confidence that it's correct. Now we need to configure Rails to run in thread-safe mode by uncommenting the following line in our config/environments/production.rb file:

Warbler/twitalytics/config/environments/production.rb
```
config.threadsafe!
```

Warbler is Rails-aware, so it will detect this configuration and implicitly create a single runtime instance of our application.

Because a development server has only one user, we'll leave it in non-thread-safe mode, but we'll set the maximum runtimes to 1 by adding the following line to the config/warbler.rb file. This will allow our application to start up faster.

Warbler/twitalytics/config/warble.rb
```
config.webxml.jruby.max.runtimes = 1
```

Let's repackage Twitalytics and run it again so we can see this in action.

```
$ warble executable war
rm -f twitalytics.war
Creating twitalytics.war
$ RAILS_ENV=development java -jar twitalytics.war
[Winstone 2012/01/12 19:47:58] - Beginning extraction from war file
[Winstone 2012/01/12 19:48:00] - WARNING: The Servlet 2.4/2.5 spec XSD was u...
[Winstone 2012/01/12 19:48:00] - No webapp classes folder found - /private/v...
[webapp 2012/01/12 19:48:00] - Info: received max runtimes = 1
[webapp 2012/01/12 19:54:44] - jruby 1.6.7 (ruby-1.8.7-p357) (2012-02-22 3e8...
[Winstone 2012/01/12 19:54:59] - Listener winstone.ajp13.Ajp13Listener not f...
[Winstone 2012/01/12 19:54:59] - Listener winstone.ssl.HttpsListener not fou...
[Winstone 2012/01/12 19:54:59] - Winstone Servlet Engine v0.9.10 running: co...
[Winstone 2012/01/12 19:54:59] - HTTP Listener started: port=8080
```

We can tell by the following line in the console output that Warbler is using a single runtime instance of our application:

```
[webapp 2012/01/12 19:48:00] - Info: received max runtimes = 1
```

We're all done! Before we move on, let's commit our changes to the warbler branch with the git add and git commit commands.

```
$ git add config/warble.rb
$ git add config/environments/production.rb
$ git commit -m "Added Warbler configuration"
```

Twitalytics is now ready to be deployed to production with Warbler.

1.5 Wrapping Up

We packaged Twitalytics into an archive file. That's a huge step for our application because it means we can deploy it to any Java servlet container. There are many possibilities, including containers that run in the cloud, containers that run on embedded devices, and containers that run on a dedicated server.

You've also learned how the JVM can simplify a Ruby architecture no matter what JRuby web framework we use. This will be important as we work our way through the book and as you continue to develop new applications on your own.

Finally, we ported Twitalytics to JRuby. The problems we solved for this application were typical of those you might see on any application you port to JRuby. You now have the knowledge you need to do this again on your own projects.

Having a JRuby application packaged into a WAR file is a good first step, but we still need to deploy it. In the coming chapters, we'll explore how to get this WAR file to our customers. But first, we need to create a production environment for it to run on.

CHAPTER 2

Creating a Deployment Environment

In this chapter, we're going to build an environment that will be used to run JRuby applications in production. The steps we'll follow are essential in preparing any server for a JRuby deployment, so you'll probably repeat them every time you set up an environment for a new customer or employer.

The environment we create will be equipped with a complete web stack including an HTTP server, a database, and the Java Virtual Machine. Deploying applications on JRuby doesn't mean we have to turn our world upside-down, so the tools we'll use to create this server may be familiar.

In Chapter 1, *Getting Started with JRuby*, on page 1, we ported Twitalytics to JRuby, and now it needs an environment to run on. At the end of this chapter, we'll have a deployment environment that's ready to take advantage of everything that JRuby has to offer. Let's get started.

2.1 Creating a Virtual Server

Deployment is the process of taking code or binaries from one environment and moving them to a another environment where they can be executed. In our case, we'll be moving code from our development machine to a production server. We already have a development environment configured, but we still need to create a production environment that can be used as the target of our deployments. To do this, we'll use Vagrant[1] and VirtualBox.[2] These tools reduce the process of provisioning a virtual server to just a few steps.

The instructions in this chapter will describe how to build an Ubuntu Linux virtual machine on a Linux or Unix host system. But you can build your

---

1. http://vagrantup.com/
2. https://www.virtualbox.org/

deployment environment with any platform you want. We'll try to address a few variations in Section 2.4, *Using Alternative Platforms*, on page 33. It's best to practice on an environment that is typical of the ones you will use in production, so you should pick one that makes sense. But the following steps will be specific to Ubuntu, VirtualBox, and Vagrant.

Let's get started by installing VirtualBox. Go to virtualbox.org,[3] and download and run the installer now. The VirtualBox user interface will open at the end of the installation, but you can close it. We're going to drive VirtualBox with Vagrant. To install Vagrant, download the binary installer for your operating system from the official website[4] and run it. The installer adds a vagrant command to our path, so we can check that both Vagrant and its connection to VirtualBox are working by running the following:

```
$ vagrant --version
Vagrant version 1.0.1
```

We could have installed the Vagrant gem, but that is not the preferred method of installation, since certain Vagrant commands do not work on JRuby. These include vagrant ssh and vagrant reload. It is possible to work around these deficiencies by running the vagrant-ssh script provided with the source code and by running vagrant halt && vagrant up, respectively, but using the binary distribution saves us a lot of time.

Now we're ready to build our deployment environment. The following command will create a fully functioning virtual machine running Ubuntu:

```
$ vagrant box add base-jruby http://files.vagrantup.com/lucid64.box
[vagrant] Downloading with Vagrant::Downloaders::HTTP...
[vagrant] Downloading box: http://files.vagrantup.com/lucid64.box
[vagrant] Copying box to temporary location...
[vagrant] Extracting box...
[vagrant] Verifying box...
[vagrant] Cleaning up downloaded box...
```

Note that the lucid64.box file is very large (about 250MB), so the previous command may take some time to run.

Next, we'll move into the twitalytics directory, which contains the Git repository we created in *Preface*, on page xi. This is where we'll keep an image of our box along with some configuration files that we want under version control. To create these configuration files, we need to run the vagrant init command with the base-jruby argument.

---

3. https://www.virtualbox.org/wiki/Downloads
4. http://downloads.vagrantup.com/tags/v1.0.1

```
$ cd ~/code/twitalytics
$ vagrant init base-jruby
```

This creates a Vagrantfile, which tells Vagrant the box that we want to interact with it when we use the vagrant command. Now we can boot our virtual machine like this:

```
$ vagrant up
[default] Importing base box 'base-jruby'...
[default] The guest additions on this VM do not match the install version of
VirtualBox! This may cause things such as forwarded ports, shared
folders, and more to not work properly. If any of those things fail on
this machine, please update the guest additions and repackage the
box.

Guest Additions Version: 4.1.0
VirtualBox Version: 4.1.8
[default] Matching MAC address for NAT networking...
[default] Clearing any previously set forwarded ports...
[default] Forwarding ports...
[default] -- 22 => 2222 (adapter 1)
[default] Creating shared folders metadata...
[default] Clearing any previously set network interfaces...
[default] Booting VM...
[default] Waiting for VM to boot. This can take a few minutes.
[default] VM booted and ready for use!
[default] Mounting shared folders...
[default] -- v-root: /vagrant
```

The VM is running! Let's log into it with the following command:

```
$ vagrant ssh
Linux lucid64 2.6.32-33-server #70-Ubuntu SMP ...
Ubuntu 10.04.3 LTS

Welcome to the Ubuntu Server!
* Documentation: http://www.ubuntu.com/server/doc
Last login: Mon Oct 17 14:24:10 2011 from 10.0.2.2
vagrant@lucid64:~$
```

The vagrant@lucid64:~$ prompt means that we are inside our virtual box.

Next, we need to update the system's package manager. Ubuntu is a Debian-based environment that uses the Advanced Packaging Tool (APT) to install software, which we can update with the following command:

```
vagrant@lucid64:~$ sudo apt-get update
```

Finally, we need to exit the virtual machine and add everything we've created to our Git repository. We'll put these changes in a new deployment branch and merge them in later, so run these commands:

```
$ git checkout -b deployment jruby
$ git add .
$ git commit -m "Added Vagrant configuration"
```

Our configuration is now under version control, and our virtual operating system is ready! Now we need to install some software on it.

2.2 Provisioning with Puppet

Puppet is a configuration management tool for Linux and Unix systems that automates the steps for building any kind of server environment. We'll be using it to provision our virtual machine with the infrastructure necessary to run a JRuby application, but it's capable of much more. In fact, Puppet is capable of automating nearly every aspect of a system administrator's job including managing user permissions, installing software, and even configuring services such as FTP and LDAP.

With Puppet, we can declaratively define the building blocks of our system. These blocks can be software, services, users, and many other things. Puppet calls each of these building blocks a *resource* and provides a *domain-specific language* (DSL) for defining them. The resources we create will be contained in manifest files that Puppet interprets into system commands.

The advantage of using Puppet over manually executing the system commands is that the Puppet DSL makes our configuration more portable and repeatable. Throughout this book, we'll be rebuilding our deployment environment more than once, and having our infrastructure defined in code will save us a lot of time. In this book, we'll only scratch the surface of how to use Puppet. If you want to learn more, the best place to start is the official documentation.[5]

Let's start by creating a directory for Puppet and our manifests.

```
$ mkdir -p puppet/manifests
```

Next, let's create a puppet/manifests/site.pp file, which will contain our primary configuration. Let's edit that file and add our first resource.

JRuby/twitalytics/puppet/manifests/site.pp
```
group { "puppet":
    ensure => "present",
}
```

The previous code ensures that a puppet group will be present on our system. If it's not present, Puppet will create it. Now let's add the site.pp manifest to

---

5. http://docs.puppetlabs.com/

our Vagrant configuration so that we can run it. Open the Vagrantfile and add the following code to the Vagrant::Config.run() block (you can delete all of the comments in it, too):

JRuby/twitalytics/Vagrantfile
```
config.vm.provision :puppet do |puppet|
  puppet.manifests_path = "puppet/manifests"
  puppet.manifest_file = "site.pp"
end
```

The previously shown configuration tells Vagrant to run Puppet after starting our virtual machine and provides the location of our manifest file. Let's test this by running the Vagrant reload command.

```
$ vagrant reload
[default] Attempting graceful shutdown of VM...
[default] VM already created. Booting if it's not already running...
[default] Clearing any previously set forwarded ports...
[default] Forwarding ports...
[default] -- 22 => 2222 (adapter 1)
[default] Creating shared folders metadata...
[default] Clearing any previously set network interfaces...
[default] Booting VM...
[default] Waiting for VM to boot. This can take a few minutes.
[default] VM booted and ready for use!
[default] Mounting shared folders...
[default] -- v-root: /vagrant
[default] -- manifests: /tmp/vagrant-puppet/manifests
[default] Running provisioner: Vagrant::Provisioners::Puppet...
[default] Running Puppet with /tmp/vagrant-puppet/manifests/site.pp...
stdin: is not a tty
notice: /Group[puppet]/ensure: created
notice: Finished catalog run in 0.05 seconds
```

Puppet created the new group. Let's add some more configuration. Open the site.pp again, and add the following exec resource, which updates our system's package manager:

JRuby/twitalytics/puppet/manifests/site.pp
```
exec { "apt-update" :
  command => "/usr/bin/apt-get update",
  require => Group[puppet]
}
Exec["apt-update"] -> Package <| |>
```

This tells Puppet to execute the provided command argument, which updates the cache for Ubuntu's Advanced Packaging Tool (APT).

The previous resource also declares a dependency on the Group resource we created earlier, which ensures that the puppet group will be created before this

Joe asks:
Is Puppet Running on JRuby?

Puppet is written in Ruby. But as you may have noticed, we are using it to install JRuby. That means Puppet is executing on the MRI runtime that was included with our Linux distribution.

We ported our application to JRuby because MRI wasn't scaling well, but that doesn't apply to our configuration management. MRI is still an excellent replacement for shell scripts as a system administration tool because it comes preloaded on many systems and the work is primarily single-threaded.

Furthermore, we've been running Puppet in stand-alone mode, which means that we simply run the Puppet scripts against our server each time it boots up. Stand-alone mode does not work on JRuby because it uses the unsupported Kernel.fork() method.

In most real-world environments, Puppet is run in a master-agent mode where a centralized management daemon (puppetmasterd) runs on a master node and the agent daemons (puppetd) run on other servers that need to use the Puppet configuration provided by the master.

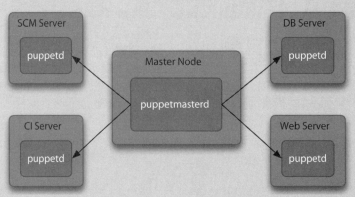

A Puppet master can be run on JRuby to improve its performance,[a] which is valuable in a large organization that needs to scale its support infrastructure. But the agents must still be run with MRI. In this book, we'll run only on MRI because we won't be using a master node.

a.   http://www.masterzen.fr/2009/05/24/puppet-and-jruby-a-love-story/

resource runs. Puppet manifests are declarative, so there is no guarantee on the order in which our resources will run unless we define explicit dependencies. In the last line, we declare that this resource must execute before any Package resources. We'll be adding a few of these resources in a moment. For now, let's run our provisioning process again. Because we've already reloaded the box, we can use the provision command to avoid restarting the whole system.

```
$ vagrant provision
[default] Running provisioner: Vagrant::Provisioners::Puppet...
[default] Running Puppet with /tmp/vagrant-puppet/manifests/site.pp...
stdin: is not a tty
notice: /Stage[main]//Exec[apt-update]/returns: executed successfully

notice: Finished catalog run in 1.13 seconds
```

The system is up-to-date. Now we're ready to install our most significant resource, the Java Virtual Machine.

Installing the Java Virtual Machine

When we discuss the Java Virtual Machine, we are usually referring to a specification that defines a core component of the Java Platform. There are many JVM implementations, but in almost every case you will want to use the HotSpot JVM. It is the most robust, well-rounded, and well-supported implementation.

To install HotSpot, you'll need to install the Java Development Kit (JDK). When doing so, be careful that you are not actually installing the Java Runtime Environment (JRE).

The JRE is a consumer environment used to run Java programs. It includes a Java Virtual Machine (JVM) but does not include a compiler or debugger. It's intended for lightweight, production-ready Java applications.

The JDK includes everything in the JRE, as well as some other tools that allow you to write, compile, monitor, and debug Java applications. It's a much bigger package as a result. You will need to install a JDK on your development machine as well as on your production server. Even though you won't be doing any actual Java development, the JDK includes components that allow server applications to run faster than if they ran on the JRE. In fact, some server frameworks actually require a JDK be present.

We can install a few different JDK packages, but in most cases we'll want to use OpenJDK. OpenJDK is an open source project that is the reference implementation for the Java Standard Edition.

Let's install OpenJDK in our virtual machine by adding it to our Puppet configuration in the puppet/manifest/site.pp file.

JRuby/twitalytics/puppet/manifests/site.pp
```
package { "openjdk-6-jdk" :
  ensure => present
}
```

This tells the system's package manager to install a package with the name of openjdk-6-jdk if it's not already present. Let's add this resource to our system by running the provisioning process again.

```
$ vagrant provision
[default] Running provisioner: Vagrant::Provisioners::Puppet...
[default] Running Puppet with /tmp/vagrant-puppet/manifests/site.pp...
stdin: is not a tty
notice: /Stage[main]//Exec[apt-update]/returns: executed successfully

notice: /Stage[main]//Package[openjdk-6-jdk]/ensure: ensure changed 'purge...
notice: Finished catalog run in 173.83 seconds
```

Puppet has installed the JDK on our virtual machine. Let's log into our box and take a look at the new platform by running these commands:

```
$ vagrant ssh
Linux lucid64 2.6.32-33-server #70-Ubuntu SMP Thu Jul 7 22:28:30 UTC 2011 ...
Ubuntu 10.04.3 LTS

Welcome to the Ubuntu Server!
 * Documentation:  http://www.ubuntu.com/server/doc
Last login: Fri Feb 10 11:36:28 2012 from 10.0.2.2
vagrant@lucid64:~$ java -version
java version "1.6.0_20"
OpenJDK Runtime Environment (IcedTea6 1.9.10) (6b20-1.9.10-0ubuntu1~10.04.3)
OpenJDK 64-Bit Server VM (build 19.0-b09, mixed mode)
```

Excellent! Now we're ready to install JRuby.

Installing JRuby

Having JRuby installed on our production server is not necessarily a requirement. Only one of the three deployment strategies we'll discuss in this book requires the installation of a JRuby runtime. The others provide it for us. But JRuby is a powerful tool that's helpful to have around, so we'll include it in our base environment.

The simplest way to get JRuby onto our virtual machine is by using the system's package manager, just as we did for the JVM. Unfortunately, most Linux distributions don't upgrade to the latest JRuby release the moment it comes out, which will leave us a few versions behind. To get the most recent version of JRuby, we'll create a Puppet module that installs it for us.

Puppet modules are used to encapsulate resources that apply to the same component. In this case, it will take a few resources to get JRuby installed on our system. So, let's create the JRuby module and its manifests directory.

```
$ mkdir -p puppet/modules/jruby/manifests
```

Next, let's add this new directory to our Vagrant configuration. Open the Vagrantfile and set the module_path attribute in our Puppet configuration.

JRuby/twitalytics/Vagrantfile

```
config.vm.provision :puppet do |puppet|
  puppet.manifests_path = "puppet/manifests"
  puppet.module_path = "puppet/modules"
  puppet.manifest_file = "site.pp"
end
```

Now let's build our JRuby manifest. Create an init.pp file in the puppet/modules/jruby/manifests/ directory, and add the following declaration to it:

JRuby/twitalytics/puppet/modules/jruby/manifests/init.pp

```
class jruby {
  $jruby_home = "/opt/jruby"
}
```

The previous code defines a class for our JRuby module. Puppet classes are collections of resources that can be applied as a unit. We'll be adding to this class, but for now we've defined a variable that contains the location where we want to install our JRuby runtime. Now let's add a resource to the class that downloads JRuby.

JRuby/twitalytics/puppet/modules/jruby/manifests/init.pp

```
exec { "download_jruby":
  command => "wget -O /tmp/jruby.tar.gz http://bit.ly/jruby-167",
  path => $path,
  unless => "ls /opt | grep jruby-1.6.7",
  require => Package["openjdk-6-jdk"]
}
```

This executes the wget command to download the JRuby binary distribution from the official JRuby website. It also checks for the /opt/jruby-1.6.7 directory, and it won't run if it already exists. Finally, it declares a dependency on the openjdk-6-jdk package resource we created earlier.

Next, we need to explode our JRuby package by adding this resource:

JRuby/twitalytics/puppet/modules/jruby/manifests/init.pp

```
exec { "unpack_jruby" :
  command => "tar -zxf /tmp/jruby.tar.gz -C /opt",
  path => $path,
  creates => "${jruby_home}-1.6.7",
  require => Exec["download_jruby"]
}
```

This extracts the contents of the file and creates the /opt/jruby-1.6.7 directory. It also declares dependencies on the earlier resources to ensure the correct order during execution.

The JRuby package contains the binaries we need, so our installation is complete. But before we move on, let's create a symbolic link to our version-specific JRuby directory.

JRuby/twitalytics/puppet/modules/jruby/manifests/init.pp
```
file { $jruby_home :
    ensure => link,
    target => "${jruby_home}-1.6.7",
    require => Exec["unpack_jruby"]
}
```

This will let us reference the JRuby directory without specifying the version.

Before we can run our new configuration, we need to include the module in our puppet/manifests/site.pp manifest. Let's open it and add this statement:

```
include jruby
```

Now we can provision our virtual machine again. We'll have to reload the system because we added the modules directory.

```
$ vagrant reload
[default] Attempting graceful shutdown of VM...
[default] VM already created. Booting if it's not already running...
[default] Clearing any previously set forwarded ports...
[default] Forwarding ports...
[default] -- 22 => 2222 (adapter 1)
[default] Creating shared folders metadata...
[default] Clearing any previously set network interfaces...
[default] Booting VM...
[default] Waiting for VM to boot. This can take a few minutes.
[default] VM booted and ready for use!
[default] Mounting shared folders...
[default] -- v-root: /vagrant
[default] -- manifests: /tmp/vagrant-puppet/manifests
[default] -- v-pp-m0: /tmp/vagrant-puppet/modules-0
[default] Running provisioner: Vagrant::Provisioners::Puppet...
[default] Running Puppet with /tmp/vagrant-puppet/manifests/site.pp...
stdin: is not a tty
notice: /Stage[main]//Exec[apt-update]/returns: executed successfully

notice: /Stage[main]/Jruby/Exec[download_jruby]/returns: executed successfully
notice: /Stage[main]/Jruby/Exec[unpack_jruby]/returns: executed successfully
notice: /Stage[main]/Jruby/File[/opt/jruby]/ensure: created

notice: Finished catalog run in 13.35 seconds
```

Excellent. We have a JRuby runtime on our machine. Let's configure the rest of the infrastructure required to run our application.

Installing the Apache HTTP Server

Throughout this book, we'll be using the Apache HTTP Server as a proxy for the web applications we deploy. There are alternatives to Apache, such as Nginx. But we've selected Apache to serve up our JRuby application because it provides some very powerful ways to integrate with the JVM web servers we'll be using. We'll demonstrate this later in the book. For now, let's create an Apache Puppet module. First, we need to create a directory for the module by running this command:

```
$ mkdir -p puppet/modules/apache2/manifests
```

Then we create an init.pp file in the new directory and add the following Apache class to it:

JRuby/twitalytics/puppet/modules/apache2/manifests/init.pp
```
class apache2 {
  package { "apache2":
    ensure => present,
  }

  service { "apache2":
    ensure => running,
    require => Package["apache2"],
  }
}
```

This will install the apache2 package and ensure that the service it creates is started.

We add the Apache module to our puppet/manifests/site.pp manifest by including this statement:

JRuby/twitalytics/puppet/manifests/site.pp
```
include apache2
```

Now we're ready to run our provisioning process again, but before we do, let's forward port 80 on our virtual machine to a port on our host. Open the Vagrantfile and add this statement to the configuration block:

JRuby/twitalytics/Vagrantfile
```
config.vm.forward_port 80, 8000
```

This will allow us to use the browser on our desktop to view Apache.

Let's run our new provisioning script and enable our forwarded port by reloading the server again.

```
$ vagrant reload
[default] Attempting graceful shutdown of VM...
```

```
[default] VM already created. Booting if it's not already running...
[default] Clearing any previously set forwarded ports...
[default] Forwarding ports...
[default] -- 22 => 2222 (adapter 1)
[default] -- 80 => 8000 (adapter 1)
[default] Creating shared folders metadata...
[default] Clearing any previously set network interfaces...
[default] Booting VM...
[default] Waiting for VM to boot. This can take a few minutes.
[default] VM booted and ready for use!
[default] Mounting shared folders...
[default] -- v-root: /vagrant
[default] -- manifests: /tmp/vagrant-puppet/manifests
[default] -- v-pp-m0: /tmp/vagrant-puppet/modules-0
[default] Running provisioner: Vagrant::Provisioners::Puppet...
[default] Running Puppet with /tmp/vagrant-puppet/manifests/site.pp...
stdin: is not a tty
notice: /Stage[main]//Exec[apt-update]/returns: executed successfully
notice: /Stage[main]/Apache2/Package[apache2]/ensure: ensure changed 'purg...
notice: Finished catalog run in 16.04 seconds
```

Apache is running on our box. Let's point our browser to http://localhost:8000, and we'll see the page shown in Figure 7, *The Apache splash page*, on page 31.

That takes care of our infrastructure's front end; now let's configure the back end.

Installing PostgreSQL

Like many web applications, Twitalytics is backed by a relational database. We'll be using PostgeSQL[6] for this book, so let's add it to our Puppet configuration by creating a new module.

There are several open source Puppet modules that install and configure PostgreSQL.[7] These modules will allow us to adjust many advanced PostgreSQL options such as security and network settings. But our installation will be very basic, so we'll define it ourselves.

Let's start by creating the module directories.

```
$ mkdir -p puppet/modules/postgres/manifests
```

Now we need to add an init.pp file to the new directory and edit it to contain the following class:

---

6. http://www.postgresql.org/
7. https://github.com/KrisBuytaert/puppet-postgres

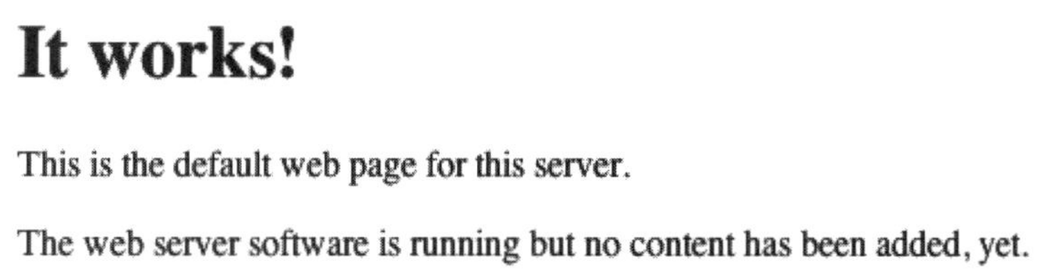

It works!

This is the default web page for this server.

The web server software is running but no content has been added, yet.

Figure 7—The Apache splash page

JRuby/twitalytics/puppet/modules/postgres/manifests/init.pp

```
class postgres {
  package { 'postgresql':
    ensure => present,
  }

  user { 'postgres':
    ensure => 'present',
    require => Package['postgresql']
  }

  group { 'postgres':
    ensure => 'present',
    require => User['postgres']
  }
}
```

This will install the postgresql package and create the matching system user and group.

Now we need to add a vagrant user to PostgreSQL and give it permissions to create databases and tables. Let's add the following two resources to the postgres class:

JRuby/twitalytics/puppet/modules/postgres/manifests/init.pp

```
exec { "createuser" :
  command => "createuser -U postgres -SdRw vagrant",
  user    => 'postgres',
  path    => $path,
  unless => "psql -c \
    \"select * from pg_user where usename='vagrant'\" | grep -c vagrant",
  require => Group['postgres']
}

exec { "psql -c \"ALTER USER vagrant WITH PASSWORD 'Passw0rd'\"":
  user    => 'postgres',
  path    => $path,
  require => Exec["createuser"]
}
```

The first resource creates the database user, and the second resource sets its password. You can use any value you prefer for the password, but remember it because we'll need it when we run our application's database settings.

Now let's include the new module in our configuration by adding the following statement to our puppet/manifests/site.pp file:

JRuby/twitalytics/puppet/manifests/site.pp
```
include postgres
```

Finally, let's provision our virtual machine again. This time we don't need to reload the system, so we can use the provision command.

```
$ vagrant provision
[default] Running provisioner: Vagrant::Provisioners::Puppet...
[default] Running Puppet with /tmp/vagrant-puppet/manifests/site.pp...
stdin: is not a tty
notice: /Stage[main]//Exec[apt-update]/returns: executed successfully
notice: /Stage[main]/Postgres/Package[postgresql]/ensure: ensure changed '...
notice: /Stage[main]/Postgres/Exec[createuser]/returns: executed successfu...
notice: /Stage[main]/Postgres/Exec[psql -c "ALTER USER vagrant WITH PASSWO...
notice: Finished catalog run in 33.45 seconds
```

When the provisioning process completes, the PostgreSQL instance will be running on our box. Let's check it out.

Log into the box with the vagrant ssh command. When you get the vagrant@lucid64:~$ prompt, run the following command to check that PostgreSQL installed correctly:

```
vagrant@lucid64:~$ psql postgres
psql (8.4.10)
Type "help" for help.

postgres=>
```

The psql command connects the local PostgreSQL client to the database. When we see the postgres=# prompt, it means that PostgreSQL is running. You can exit the psql client by entering \q at the prompt.

Our deployment environment is now complete, but before we move on, we need to save all the work we've done. After exiting the virtual machine, we can add our configuration to the Git repository with these commands:

```
$ git add puppet
$ git add Vagrantfile
$ git commit -m "Added Puppet configuration"
```

Now we'll merge these changes into our jruby and warbler branches.

```
$ git checkout jruby
Switched to branch 'jruby'
$ git merge deployment
...
 create mode 100644 Vagrantfile
 create mode 100644 puppet/manifests/site.pp
 create mode 100644 puppet/modules/apache2/manifests/init.pp
 create mode 100644 puppet/modules/jruby/manifests/init.pp
 create mode 100644 puppet/modules/postgres/manifests/init.pp
$ git checkout warbler
Switched to branch 'warbler'
$ git merge jruby
...
 create mode 100644 Vagrantfile
 create mode 100644 puppet/manifests/site.pp
 create mode 100644 puppet/modules/apache2/manifests/init.pp
 create mode 100644 puppet/modules/jruby/manifests/init.pp
 create mode 100644 puppet/modules/postgres/manifests/init.pp
```

Our configuration has been saved and propagated to our other branches. But we also want to save our virtual machine. Let's use Vagrant to do that.

2.3 Packaging the Deployment Environment

Vagrant allows us to package the environment we've created into a reusable image by running the following command:

```
$ vagrant package --output base-jruby.box
[default] Clearing any previously set forwarded ports...
[default] Creating temporary directory for export...
[default] Exporting VM...
[default] Compressing package to: ~/code/twitalytics/base-jruby.box
```

This will create a base-jruby.box file in the current directory that contains an image of the virtual machine. We won't commit this to version control because it's too big. That's why the .gitignore file in our source code already has it listed.

In this book, you'll learn about three deployment techniques. For each technique, we'll use base-jruby.box as the basis for creating a new deployment target.

2.4 Using Alternative Platforms

The steps in this chapter are specific to the Vagrant box we created. They also assume that they are being followed on a Linux or Unix machine. As a result, many of the previous commands are specific to Linux, Unix, and even Ubuntu.

But one of the advantages of JRuby is its portability. That means we could build a system very similar to the one we built in this chapter with many different platforms, including Windows. In fact, the recommended way to use Vagrant on Windows without a binary installer is with JRuby.

In this section, we'll try to address a few common scenarios you might encounter when creating an alternative environment.

Accessing the Server

Some of the steps described earlier require shell access to the guest operating system. As long as your guest operating system is based on Linux or Unix, then these steps should remain the same. But if the host operating system is Windows, we'll need to use a different method to access our guest.

Fortunately, Vagrant provides special support for PuTTY, a free Telnet and SSH client for Windows. You'll need to download and install PuTTY from the official website[8] and follow the instructions for configuring it on the Vagrant website.[9]

By accessing the guest with PuTTY, a Windows host should be able to execute all of the regular Vagrant steps in this chapter.

Installing the JVM

One of the steps in this chapter required that we install a JDK. We chose OpenJDK for Ubuntu, but that may not be the best choice for other systems.

For Macs, Apple distributes its own JDK with a Mac OS X port of the HotSpot JVM. If you're using a Windows environment, you'll want to install the Oracle JDK. The Oracle JDK is a commercial packaging of OpenJDK that includes a few closed source components. You can download and run the binary installer from the Oracle website.[10] After the installation has completed, you'll need to set the JAVA_HOME variable like this (note that the exact path will vary based on the version you installed):

```
C:\> SET JAVA_HOME="C:\Program Files\Java\jdk1.6.0_27"
```

Portability is one of Java's strong points, so you should be able to find a JVM for any environment you need to deploy to, even if it's a phone.[11]

---

8. http://www.chiark.greenend.org.uk/~sgtatham/putty/download.html

9. http://vagrantup.com/v1/docs/getting-started/ssh.html

10. http://www.oracle.com/technetwork/java/javase/downloads/index.html

11. http://www.dalvikvm.com/

Creating a Machine Image

Vagrant allowed us to package our virtual machine in a reusable file. If your alternative environment does not have a similar feature, then you may want to create a machine image. A machine image is a snapshot of a virtual environment that can be reloaded without reinstalling or configuring its components. For this reason it's often called a software *appliance*.

One popular deployment environment is Amazon's Elastic Compute Cloud (EC2). Amazon provides detailed instructions for how to create and restore EC2 machine images.[12]

If creating a machine image is not possible, you can always repeat these steps for each of the deployment strategies that will be presented in this book. As another option, you can clean up after each of the deployment techniques. That will require you to uninstall or reconfigure any software that may have been used in a particular chapter.

2.5 Wrapping Up

We've created an environment that can be used to run Twitalytics and other JRuby applications in production. We've prepared it with the essential components of a web stack, so it's likely that we'll repeat these steps each time we encounter a new customer or employer.

We've also set up Puppet, which will allow us to add new components to our infrastructure without running a bunch of commands. When we create a second instance of this environment, maybe for a cluster, we won't have to do much work. We'll start with our base box, and Puppet will provision the rest of it for us.

Let's move on and deploy a JRuby application.

---

12. http://aws.amazon.com/amis

CHAPTER 3

Deploying an Archive File

Wouldn't it be nice if we could deploy an entire application as a single file? That's exactly what Warbler does by packaging our code into a web archive (WAR) file. In Chapter 1, *Getting Started with JRuby*, on page 1, you learned how to create this package, but now we need to deploy it.

Traditional Ruby application deployment usually involves a step where a repository or directory of source files is copied to a server. Tools like Capistrano[1] were built to help with this task, but they have their drawbacks.

Copying a directory of source files onto a server means that the owner of the target machine is exposed to your application files and directory structure. This is particularly problematic when the owner isn't you. Permissions can be set wrong if a file extension or directory was missed by a command. In the worst case, parts of the application can be deleted or overwritten accidentally. At the very least, you may not want the owner of the target machine to have access to your source code for reasons of propriety.

WAR files are a simple solution to these problems. They provide a modular, portable, and easy-to-distribute package for our applications. But they can't run inside traditional Ruby web servers. Instead, WAR files need to run inside Java-based containers that understand their format. In *Getting Started with JRuby*, we embedded a server like this into our archive file so that we could run it in stand-alone mode. This was convenient for testing our archive, but that isn't how we want to deploy our application to production. Instead, we want to deploy our WAR file to a free-standing container, which will provide more flexibility and better performance than our embedded container.

---

1. https://github.com/capistrano/capistrano

In this chapter, you'll learn about the Apache Tomcat[2] web server, which is one of the most mature and widely adopted web servers available.[3] We'll install Tomcat on a production server and write a script that deploys the WAR file we created in the previous chapter to this new container.

Deploying a WAR file does not require special tools like Capistrano, which reduce the portability and flexibility of the deployment process. We'll use SSH to deploy the Twitalytics WAR file to a Linux server, but we could just as easily deploy it to a Windows server using FTP. In fact, we can deploy a WAR file using any remote file transfer protocol.

But before we can deploy, we'll need to create an environment for Twitalytics to run on.

3.1 Provisioning a Server

We're going to create a virtual server based on the one we started in Chapter 2, *Creating a Deployment Environment*, on page 19. Let's change our location to the twitalytics directory and use the vagrant box command to add a new instance.

```
$ cd ~/code/twitalytics
$ git checkout warbler
$ vagrant box add warbler base-jruby.box
[vagrant] Downloading with Vagrant::Downloaders::File...
[vagrant] Copying box to temporary location...
[vagrant] Extracting box...
[vagrant] Verifying box...
[vagrant] Cleaning up downloaded box...
```

This created a new virtual machine that we can execute our Puppet scripts against. But first, we need to reconfigure our Vagrantfile. Open the file and adjust the config.vm.box attribute so the code looks like this:

Warbler/twitalytics/Vagrantfile
```
Vagrant::Config.run do |config|
  config.vm.box = "warbler"
  config.vm.forward_port 80, 8000
  config.vm.provision :puppet do |puppet|
    puppet.manifests_path = "puppet/manifests"
    puppet.module_path = "puppet/modules"
    puppet.manifest_file = "site.pp"
  end
end
```

---

2. http://tomcat.apache.org/
3. http://wiki.apache.org/tomcat/PoweredBy

Now the configuration references the warbler instance we created earlier.

Next, let's boot and provision the server.

```
$ vagrant up
[default] Importing base box 'warbler'...
...
[default] Booting VM...
[default] Waiting for VM to boot. This can take a few minutes.
...
[default] Running provisioner: Vagrant::Provisioners::Puppet...
[default] Running Puppet with site.pp...
...
[default] notice: Finished catalog run in 56.23 seconds
```

Now that our warbler virtual machine is ready, we can install our web server.

3.2 Installing Apache Tomcat

As we discussed earlier in the chapter, we're going to use Tomcat to serve up our WAR file. Tomcat provides an implementation of the Java Servlet API, which is why it's often called a *servlet container*. The Servlet API defines a protocol for receiving and responding to requests (usually from the Web). This makes its role very similar to Rack.

But Twitalytics isn't written against the Java Servlet API. It's a Rails application that is designed to run on Rack. That's where jruby-rack comes in. The jruby-rack gem is an adapter between the Rack interface and the Servlet interface. This allows our Rack-based application to run within a Java servlet container.

Warbler has already bundled the jruby-rack gem into our WAR file, so we can take advantage of it without any additional configuration. The resulting architecture is pictured in Figure 8, *Architecture of a JRuby Rack application*, on page 40.

Apache Tomcat is one of the best servlet containers out there. It's well-supported, is stable, and is in widespread use by hundreds of organizations.[4]

We're going to use Puppet to install Tomcat for the same reasons we installed Apache and PostgreSQL with Puppet in Chapter 2, *Creating a Deployment Environment*, on page 19. Let's start by creating a new module directory.

```
$ mkdir -p puppet/modules/tomcat6/manifests
```

In the new directory, let's create an init.pp file and add this class to it:

---

4.   http://wiki.apache.org/tomcat/PoweredBy

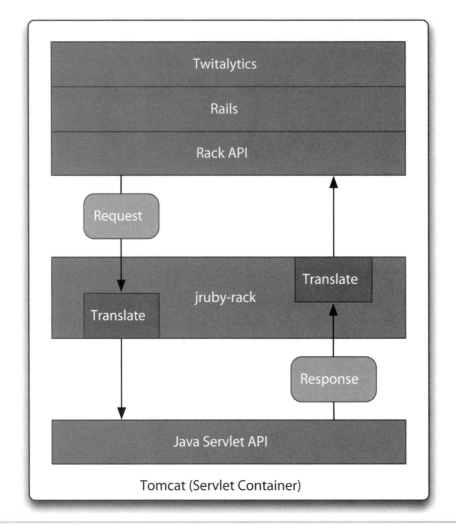

Figure 8—Architecture of a JRuby Rack application

Warbler/twitalytics/puppet/modules/tomcat6/manifests/init.pp

```
class tomcat6 {
  package { "tomcat6" :
    ensure => present
  }

  service { "tomcat6" :
    ensure => running,
    require => Package["tomcat6"]
  }
}
```

The previous code installs the tomcat6 package with the operating system's package manager. In our case, it's using APT because we're running Ubuntu. Then, it starts Tomcat as a background service.

Next, we need to include this module in our puppet/manifests/site.pp manifest by adding the following statement:

Warbler/twitalytics/puppet/manifests/site.pp
```
include tomcat6
```

Now we're ready to provision the server again. But first, let's forward port 8080 on our guest OS to a port on our host OS. This will allow us to access Tomcat from the browser on our host system. Edit the Vagrantfile again, and add this line to the configuration block:

Warbler/twitalytics/Vagrantfile
```
config.vm.forward_port 8080, 8888
```

Finally, let's reload the virtual machine.

```
$ vagrant reload
[default] Attempting graceful shutdown of VM...
[default] VM already created. Booting if it's not already running...
[default] Clearing any previously set forwarded ports...
[default] Forwarding ports...
[default] -- 22 => 2222 (adapter 1)
[default] -- 80 => 8000 (adapter 1)
[default] -- 8080 => 8888 (adapter 1)
[default] Creating shared folders metadata...
[default] Clearing any previously set network interfaces...
[default] Booting VM...
[default] Waiting for VM to boot. This can take a few minutes.
[default] VM booted and ready for use!
[default] Mounting shared folders...
[default] -- v-root: /vagrant
[default] -- manifests: /tmp/vagrant-puppet/manifests
[default] -- v-pp-m0: /tmp/vagrant-puppet/modules-0
[default] Running provisioner: Vagrant::Provisioners::Puppet...
[default] Running Puppet with /tmp/vagrant-puppet/manifests/site.pp...
stdin: is not a tty
notice: /Stage[main]//Exec[apt-update]/returns: executed successfully
notice: /Stage[main]/Tomcat6/Package[tomcat6]/ensure: ensure changed 'purged...
notice: /Stage[main]/Postgres/Exec[psql -c "ALTER USER vagrant WITH PASSWORD...
notice: Finished catalog run in 30.78 seconds
```

The output shown earlier tells us that Puppet successfully installed the Tomcat service. Let's verify it by pointing a browser to http://localhost:8888, where we'll see a page that looks like Figure 9, *The Tomcat splash page*, on page 42.

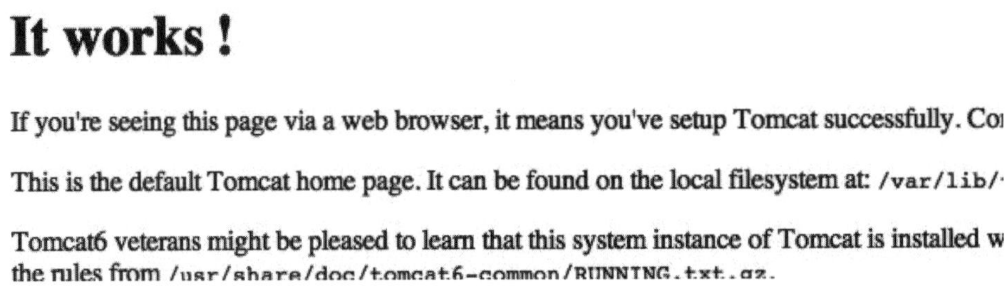

It works !

If you're seeing this page via a web browser, it means you've setup Tomcat successfully. Co

This is the default Tomcat home page. It can be found on the local filesystem at: /var/lib/

Tomcat6 veterans might be pleased to learn that this system instance of Tomcat is installed w
the rules from /usr/share/doc/tomcat6-common/RUNNING.txt.gz.

Figure 9—The Tomcat splash page

When we installed Tomcat, a few directories were created. The following is how they appear on our Vagrant machine:

```
/var/lib/tomcat6/
|-- common/
|-- conf/
|-- logs/
|-- shared/
|-- webapps/
`-- work/
```

We're mainly interested in three of these directories. The first is the conf directory. It contains a server.xml file, which is used to configure nearly everything about our container. We can use it to set the hostname and port that Tomcat will listen on. Or we can specify how the server shuts down and add life-cycle listeners. If you want to become a Tomcat power user, this is the place to start. But for Twitalytics, and most applications, we won't need to change any of it.

Another important directory is /var/lib/tomcat6/logs, which contains the server and application log files. Inside that directory is a file called catalina.out that contains information of the container and the status of any deployments. Next to that file will be a localhost-<date>.log file that contains the logging output of our application.

A more important location is the webapps/ directory. This is where we will drop our WAR file. Tomcat listens to this directory and immediately deploys any web applications it finds.

Let's write a deployment script that moves our WAR file from the machine it was created on to the webapps/ directory.

> ## Installing Tomcat Without Puppet
>
> If you're not using Vagrant and Puppet with us, you'll need to install Tomcat manually. To do this, download the binary package from the Tomcat website,[a] unpack it, and run the $TOMCAT_HOME/bin/startup.sh script. This will start the server in the same way as our Puppet configuration did.
>
> Tomcat even includes a binary installer for Windows that creates a service for you.
>
> ---
>
> a. http://tomcat.apache.org/download-60.cgi

3.3 Creating the Deployment Script

A deployment script is the part of any configuration that will probably differ the most from system to system. For Twitalytics, we're going to create a Rake task that packages the WAR file and copies it to the production server. In our example, we'll run it from our development machine. This isn't perfect, but it will demonstrate the essential steps in any WAR file deployment strategy, which are as follows:

1. Transfer the archive file to the production server.
2. Optionally run migrations against the production database.
3. Deploy the archive file to the web server.

Because our code is packaged into a single file, the first and third steps don't require much effort. We don't have to use Capistrano or Git, so there is nothing to configure. But having an archive file makes the second step more difficult.

Unlike Capistrano, Warbler doesn't mirror our development environment on the production server. As we discussed in Chapter 1, *Getting Started with JRuby*, on page 1, this might be a good feature. But it means that we have to execute migrations in a different way.

One approach is to create a Tomcat life-cycle listener that runs migrations from the exploded WAR file before starting the application. But this requires some Java code and a custom web.xml file (the deployment descriptor for a WAR file). A better strategy for us is to manually explode the WAR file and run migrations before deploying it. We'll do this as part of our Rake task.

Before we can build our Rake task, we need to include some new dependencies. Let's open the project's Gemfile and add this group:

Warbler/twitalytics/Gemfile

```
group :deploy do
  gem "net-ssh", :require => "net/ssh"
  gem "net-scp", :require => "net/scp"
  gem "warbler", "1.3.4"
end
```

Save the file and run bundle install to fetch the new dependencies.

Next, let's create a lib/tasks/deploy.rake file and edit it. We'll add the following statements, which load the gem group we just added:

Warbler/twitalytics/lib/tasks/deploy.rake

```
require 'bundler'
Bundler.require(:deploy)
```

Next, we need to add some helpers that will be used by our deployment script. The first helper will serve the same purpose as our vagrant ssh command, but in a cross-platform friendly way (including Windows). To create it, add the following code to the end of the script:

Warbler/twitalytics/lib/tasks/deploy.rake

```
SSH_KEY = "~/.vagrant.d/insecure_private_key"

def with_ssh
  Net::SSH.start("localhost", "vagrant", {
      :port => 2222, :keys => [SSH_KEY]
  }) do |ssh|
    yield ssh
  end
end
```

The with_ssh() method will allow us to execute commands on the remote server. It uses the vagrant user and the SSH key provided by Vagrant to log into the box.

The next helper method will allow us to copy files to the remote server. To create it, add the following code to the end of the script:

Warbler/twitalytics/lib/tasks/deploy.rake

```
def scp_upload(local_file, remote_file)
  Net::SCP.upload!("localhost", "vagrant", local_file, remote_file, {
      :ssh => {:port => 2222, :keys => [SSH_KEY]}
  }) do |ch, name, sent, total|
    print "\rCopying #{name}: #{sent}/#{total}"
  end; print "\n"
end
```

The scp_upload(local_file, remote_file) method uses the Secure Copy (SCP) protocol to transfer files to the Vagrant box.

In practice, these helpers should be more robust. They would probably configure the host and username based on the RAILS_ENV we pass to the script. But we're going to live on the edge. We'll only be deploying directly from development to production.

Next, we need to create a deployment task that will package our code into a WAR file and push it to our server. We'll start by creating the WAR file. Add the following code to the script:

```
Warbler/twitalytics/lib/tasks/deploy.rake
namespace :deploy do
  desc "Package the application into a WAR file and deploy it"
  task :war do
    Warbler::Task.new(:warble)
    Rake::Task['warble'].invoke
  end
end
```

This task creates a *warble* task on the fly and invokes it. This allows us to seamlessly switch between the warble command we've been using and our new Rake task without having the two mechanism conflict. We can test it by saving the file and running the following command from the project's root directory:

```
$ rake deploy:war
rm -f twitalytics.war
Creating twitalytics.war
```

Good. But our task isn't doing any more than the warble command was doing. We need to fill it out by adding the following code after the line that invokes the *warble* task:

```
Warbler/twitalytics/lib/tasks/deploy.rake
with_ssh do |ssh|
  ssh.exec! "mkdir -p deploy/"
  ssh.exec! "rm -rf deploy/*"
end
```

This will prepare a deploy directory on our production server by creating it if it doesn't exist and removing any residual files if it does exist. We'll be copying our WAR file to this directory before deploying it. To do that, add this statement immediately after the last one:

```
Warbler/twitalytics/lib/tasks/deploy.rake
scp_upload("twitalytics.war", "deploy/")
```

To test this, we need to make sure our virtual server is running by executing this command:

```
$ vagrant status
Current VM states:

default                    running

The VM is running. To stop this VM, you can run `vagrant halt` to
shut it down forcefully, or you can run `vagrant suspend` to simply
suspend the virtual machine. In either case, to restart it again,
simply run `vagrant up`.
```

If the status is different from the previous output, run the vagrant up command. With the server running, we can execute our Rake task again.

```
$ rake deploy:war
rm -f twitalytics.war
Creating twitalytics.war
Copying twitalytics.war: 81839088/81839088
```

At this point, the twitalytics.war file has been copied to the deploy directory on our server, but now we need the ability to run Rake tasks from within our WAR file. To do that, we'll use the warbler-exec gem.

The warbler-exec gem[5] is a simple tool that extracts the contents of a WAR file and allows us to run a command within the context of those contents. We can do this with a command in the following form:

```
$ warbler-exec <war-file> <command> <command-args>
```

We're going to use this tool to run our Rake migrations task, so we'll need to include both our Rakefile and the rake executable in our WAR file. To do this, we'll first need to run Bundler with the --binstubs option, like this:

```
$ bundle install --binstubs
```

This will create a bin directory in our application that contains all the executable scripts from our gem files. Running these scripts is analogous to running bundle exec <script>.

Warbler won't include our bin directory or Rakefile in the WAR by default, so we'll need to add these lines to our config/warble.rb file:

Warbler/twitalytics/config/warble.rb
```
config.dirs << "bin"
config.includes = FileList["Rakefile"]
```

Next, we need to use the warbler-exec tool in our deploy process to run the migrations. We can do that by adding this code to the task:

---

5.   https://github.com/jkutner/warbler-exec

Warbler/twitalytics/lib/tasks/deploy.rake

```
with_ssh do |ssh|
  ssh.exec <<-SH do |ch, stream, data|
    cd deploy
    export PATH=$PATH:/opt/jruby/bin
    export RAILS_ENV=production
    sudo jgem install warbler-exec
    jruby -S warbler-exec twitalytics.war bin/rake db:migrate
  SH
    print data
  end
end
```

This will install the warbler-exec gem and use it to run the application's Rake migrate task.

Let's see how we're doing by running the Rake task again.

```
$ rake deploy:war
rm -f twitalytics.war
Creating twitalytics.war
Copying twitalytics.war: 81839088/81839088
Successfully installed rubyzip-0.9.6.1
Successfully installed warbler-exec-0.1.0
2 gems installed
==  CreateStatuses: migrating ====================================================
-- create_table(:statuses)
   -> 0.0040s
   -> 0 rows
==  CreateStatuses: migrated (0.0060s) ==========================================

==  CreateAnalytics: migrating ===================================================
-- create_table(:analytics)
   -> 0.0040s
   -> 1 rows
==  CreateAnalytics: migrated (0.0040s) =========================================
```

Excellent. The database has been migrated. Now we can deploy the WAR file to Tomcat by adding this command:

Warbler/twitalytics/lib/tasks/deploy.rake

```
with_ssh do |ssh|
  ssh.exec! "sudo mv deploy/twitalytics.war /var/lib/tomcat6/webapps/"
  puts 'Deployment complete!'
end
```

Tomcat will detect that a new WAR file has been dropped into its webapps directory. Then it will automatically undeploy the old application, if one exists, and replace it with the new one.

Let's test it. Save the file and run the task again.

```
$ rake deploy:war
rm -f twitalytics.war
Creating twitalytics.war
Copying twitalytics.war: 81839088/81839088
Successfully installed warbler-exec-0.1.0
1 gem installed
Deployment complete!
```

Point your browser to http://localhost:8888/twitalytics, and you'll see the Twitalytics dashboard. Tomcat deployed our application under the twitalytics/ context path because that was the name of our WAR file. This is a configurable option, but we'll stick with the default. However, that will have an impact on the Rails asset pipeline.

3.4 Using Precompiled Assets with Warbler

Ruby on Rails version 3.1 introduced a feature called the *asset pipeline*. An asset is a style sheet, JavaScript file, or image that is served as part of the static content for a website. The asset pipeline is a framework to concatenate, minify, and compress these assets so they can be loaded faster.

When we use our Rails application in development, it compiles assets as needed. In production, we don't want to incur this overhead, so we'll want to precompile our assets prior to deployment. Traditional Ruby applications have the choice of precompiling assets on the production server or precompiling them locally and deploying them with the rest of the application. With Warbler, we can precompile the assets locally and package them into our WAR file with the rest of our content.

Twitalytics has disabled the asset pipeline by default, so we need to enable it by opening the config/application.rb file and replacing the statement that sets config.assets.enabled to false with these lines of code:

Warbler/assetpipeline/config/application.rb
```
config.assets.enabled = true
config.assets.initialize_on_precompile = false
```

The first statement enables the asset pipeline, and the second statement prevents Rails from initializing during the compilation process. This is necessary because precompilation is done in the production Rails environment, and it will fail if it does not have access to the production database, which we have not made available to our development environment.

Next, we'll open the config/environments/production.rb file and set the asset host by adding this line to it:

```
Warbler/assetpipeline/config/environments/production.rb
config.action_controller.asset_host = "/twitalytics"
```

This is necessary because we are deploying our application under the /twitalytics context (that's why we accessed the application at http://localhost:8888/twitalytics). But Rails looks for our assets under the /assets path by default. Setting the asset host will force it to look for them under the /twitalytics/assets path.

We also need to replace this line in the app/views/layout/application.html.erb file:

```
Warbler/twitalytics/app/views/layouts/application.html.erb
<%= javascript_include_tag "jquery", "rails" %>
```

with the following line, which includes the JavaScript from the asset pipeline instead of the previous static JavaScript files:

```
Warbler/assetpipeline/app/views/layouts/application.html.erb
<%= javascript_include_tag "application" %>
```

Now we can precompile our assets with the Rake task from Rails.

```
$ rake assets:precompile
~/.rvm/rubies/jruby-1.6.7/bin/jruby ~/.rvm/gems/jruby-1.6.7/bin/rake assets:pre
compile:all RAILS_ENV=production RAILS_GROUPS=assets
```

The assets will be compiled using our embedded JavaScript interpreter, therubyrhino, which we added to our Gemfile in Chapter 1, *Getting Started with JRuby*, on page 1. The resulting artifacts will be placed in the public/assets directory, which will be packaged into the WAR file when we run our deployment task again.

```
$ rake deploy:war
rm -f twitalytics.war
Creating twitalytics.war
Copying twitalytics.war: 82170669/82170669
Successfully installed warbler-exec-0.1.0
1 gem installed
Deployment complete!
```

The only evidence of our configuration change will be the size of the WAR file. You'll notice that it's slightly larger than it was before.

Now let's commit all of the changes we've made in this chapter to our warbler branch by running these commands:

```
$ git add .
$ git commit -m "prepared for war file deployment"
```

Our deployment of the Twitalytics web application on JRuby is complete. We've packaged the application into a WAR file, and we are running it on a dedicated server. But there are other components of Twitalytics that have not been incorporated.

Twitalytics has some tasks that need to run in the background, and some of them need to run at regular intervals. We haven't included these in the deployment steps because their setup will remain entirely the same as the MRI version of Twitalytics. We would probably use Resque or DelayedJob for the background tasks and cron to schedule the recurring ones. Warbler can't help us there.

But serving all of our site's web requests with a single process is still a huge improvement over the old infrastructure. Unfortunately, setting up the dedicated server is a lot of work. You may find that you don't have the time or resources to support this kind of deployment. If that's the case, then a managed cloud platform might be a better solution.

3.5 Deploying to the Cloud

This chapter has focused exclusively on deployment to a dedicated server up to this point. But there are many deployment options that don't require us to configure everything from the operating system up. In this section, you'll learn how to deploy a WAR file to a managed shared host. There are many candidates that could host our application, including Google AppEngine and Heroku. But we'll be using CloudBees, a Java-based host that is JRuby friendly.[6]

CloudBees is a platform as a service (PaaS) for building, testing, and running Java-based applications. We'll use only the part that runs applications in this book, but you could build and test Twitalytics with the platform, too.

Let's begin by creating a CloudBees account. Browse to the sign-up page,[7] and fill in some basic information. Once we finish signing up, it will bring us to the CloudBees dashboard.

From the dashboard, we need to subscribe our account to the RUN@Cloud application and database services, which can be enabled from the subscriptions page.[8] Both of these services have free offerings that will be sufficient for our usage.

---

6. http://www.cloudbees.com/
7. https://grandcentral.cloudbees.com/account/signup
8. https://grandcentral.cloudbees.com/subscriptions

Now that we are subscribed to the appropriate services, we can use the CloudBees command-line tool to finish our configuration. The tool is part of the CloudBees SDK, so let's install that next. For Linux and Unix systems (including Mac OS X), we need to run these commands:

```
$ curl -L cloudbees-downloads.s3.amazonaws.com/sdk/cloudbees-sdk-0.7.3-dist.zip
$ unzip cloudbees-sdk-0.7.3-dist.zip -d ~/bees_sdk
```

Now we need to set the BEES_HOME environment variable and add its bin directory to our path. We can do this by adding the following lines to our .profile file:

```
export BEES_HOME=~/bees_sdk/cloudbees-sdk-0.7.3
export PATH=$PATH:$BEES_HOME
```

Finally, test it by running the bees command.

```
$ bees help deploy
# CloudBees SDK version: 0.7.3
usage: bees deploy [options]
 -a,--appid <arg>         CloudBees application ID
 -b,--baseDir <arg>       Base directory (default: '.')
 -d,--delta <arg>         true to enable, false to disable delta upload
                          (default: true)
 -e,--environment <arg>   Environment configurations to deploy
 -k,--key <arg>           CloudBees API key
 -m,--message <arg>       Message describing the deployment
 -s,--secret <arg>        CloudBees API secret
 -t,--type <arg>          deployment container type
 -v,--verbose             verbose output
```

We'll be using the bees deploy command in just a moment, but first we need to create a database. To do this, we'll use the bees db:create command and provide it the name of our database, which we'll call *twitalytics*.

```
$ bees db:create twitalytics
# CloudBees SDK version: 0.7.3
Database Username (must be unique): twitalytics123
Database Password: ********
database created: twitalytics
```

The command will prompt us for a username and password, which will be used to create an account for our database. The username must be universally unique, so you'll have to pick something other than the one shown earlier.

Next, let's configure our application to use the new database. To do this, we'll need the address of the instance we created. We can get this by running the bees db:list command and specifying the verbose option:

```
$ bees db:list -v
# CloudBees SDK version: 0.7.3
API call: https://api.cloudbees.com/api?timestamp=1322016054&v=1.0&api_key=...
xml response: <?xml version="1.0" encoding="UTF-8"?>
<DatabaseListResponse>
  <databases>
    <DatabaseInfo>
      <name>twitalytics</name>
      <owner>twitalytics123</owner>
      <username>twitalytics123</username>
      <created>2011-11-07T22:26:23+00:00</created>
      <status>active</status>
      <master>ec2-0-0-0-0.compute-1.amazonaws.com</master>
      <slaves/>
      <port>3306</port>
  </databases>
</DatabaseListResponse>
Databases:
twitalytics123/twitalytics
```

The previous command has returned an XML response with the connection parameters for our database. We'll be using the <master> element and the <port> element, so make note of them.

Next, let's open the config/database.yml file and replace the production: element with something like the following code. Your username and password will be the same as the ones you entered when creating the earlier database. The hostname and port will be the values from the <master> element and the <port> element, respectively.

Warbler/cloudbees/config/database.yml
```
production:
  adapter: mysql
  host: ec2-0-0-0-0.compute-1.amazonaws.com
  port: 3306
  database: yourDatabaseName
  username: yourAccount
  password: ********
```

As you probably noticed, we're using MySQL instead of PostgreSQL, so we'll have to update our gem dependencies. Let's replace the :production group in our Gemfile with the following code and run bundle install:

Warbler/cloudbees/Gemfile
```
group :production do
  gem 'jdbc-mysql'
end
```

Now we can run our migrations.

```
$ rake db:migrate RAILS_ENV=production
==  CreateStatuses: migrating ==================================================
-- create_table(:statuses)
   -> 0.0040s
   -> 0 rows
==  CreateStatuses: migrated (0.0060s) =========================================

==  CreateAnalytics: migrating =================================================
-- create_table(:analytics)
   -> 0.0040s
   -> 1 rows
==  CreateAnalytics: migrated (0.0040s) ========================================
```

That means our database is working!

We're ready to deploy our application. Let's rebuild the twitalytics.war file using the warble command.

```
$ warble war
rm -f twitalytics.war
Creating twitalytics.war
```

Next, let's deploy the application by using the bees deploy command instead of our custom Rake task.

```
$ bees deploy twitalytics.war -appid yourAccount/twitalytics
# CloudBees SDK version: 0.7.3
Deploying application yourAccount/twitalytics (environment: ): twitalytics.war
......................uploaded 25%
......................uploaded 50%
......................uploaded 75%
......................upload completed
deploying application to server(s)...
Application yourAccount/twitalytics deployed: http://yourAccount.twitalytics ...
```

The first time we run the previous command, it will create a new application with the appid we provide. Subsequent runs will deploy the new version of the application in place of the existing version.

The last line of the console output shown previously contains a URL to the application. Point a browser to that location, and you'll see Twitalytics.

Those are the essentials of the CloudBees SDK. There are other tools that allow you to see the server's log file, run the application locally, and more. Run the bees help to get a complete list.

Before we move on, let's commit these changes to a cloudbees Git branch by running these commands:

```
$ git checkout -b cloudbees
M Gemfile
M config/database.yml
Switched to a new branch 'cloudbees'
$ git add .
$ git commit -m "ported to cloudbees"
```

CloudBees is a great solution if you are open to a managed shared host. You don't have to configure a dedicated server environment and make sure it's administered correctly. But deploying a WAR file to the cloud doesn't solve all of our problems. We still need to run background tasks and scheduled jobs.

Because CloudBees is first and foremost a Java platform, it doesn't have direct support for external processes that run jobs and tasks because Java applications don't usually need that. We could sidestep this by wrapping our external processes in their own web application and deploying it to CloudBees. But we would have to fight with frameworks like Resque, which naively assume they are the only thing in the process.

If your application needs to make heavy use of background tasks and scheduled jobs, like Twitalytics does, then you'll find that WAR file deployment is not the best solution. In *Creating a Trinidad Application* and *Creating a TorqueBox Application*, you'll learn about two JRuby servers that provide tools for these kinds of asynchronous tasks. There are even cloud-based platforms to host the deployment of these other solutions, which we'll discuss later in the book.

3.6 Wrapping Up

In this chapter, we've configured our deployment environment and created deployment scripts so that we can deploy the WAR file we created in Chapter 1, *Getting Started with JRuby*, on page 1. We deployed it to a dedicated server but also showed how it could be deployed to a cloud server. This was the most direct way to get Twitalytics running on JRuby.

Unfortunately, there are downsides to this style of deployment. Our development environment is very different from our production environment. We're probably using WEBrick as we write our code to get instant feedback after our changes. We could set up a servlet container on our development machines and deploy the WAR file as we write and test code. But we would lose the instant feedback that Rubyists are so familiar with.

Even worse, we haven't helped our background tasks and scheduled jobs. They still have to run in a separate process (even if they are running on JRuby). We are eventually going to outgrow Warbler.

Fortunately, there are other options for JRuby deployment. Now that we've proven our application can work with JRuby, it's time to go a step further. Let's deploy Twitalytics to an environment that gives us most of the advantages that Warbler gave us but uses a more traditional deployment strategy.

CHAPTER 4

Creating a Trinidad Application

To make our JRuby deployment feel more natural to Rubyists, we're going to port our application to Trinidad.[1] Trinidad is a lightweight server that runs Rails and Rack applications within an embedded Apache Tomcat[2] container without requiring a WAR file.

Trinidad works much like other Ruby web servers, so if you are familiar with Mongrel,[3] Thin,[4] or Unicorn,[5] you'll find that Trinidad fits right into your workflow. For an existing application like Twitalytics, this will help developers who are already working on it and want to continue using the tools they are familiar with.

But Trinidad differs from traditional Ruby web servers in its ability to embed many kinds of background processes into our application runtime. Message queues and scheduled jobs won't require dozens of processes like they do with MRI-based applications. This will further improve the infrastructure we began to simplify in the previous chapter.

In Chapter 1, *Getting Started with JRuby*, on page 1, we ported Twitalytics to JRuby, but we were packaging everything into an archive file rather than deploying with Capistrano or pushing from a Git repository. There are advantages to deploying an archive file, but we would like to keep the Twitalytics deployment as traditional as possible in order to keep the productivity of our development team high. Let's discuss what this means.

---

1. https://github.com/trinidad/trinidad
2. http://tomcat.apache.org/
3. http://rubyforge.org/projects/mongrel/
4. http://code.macournoyer.com/thin/
5. https://github.com/defunkt/unicorn

4.1 What Is Traditional Deployment?

Traditional Ruby deployment uses a type of runtime architecture that handles HTTP requests by placing a proxy in front of a pool of application instances. In Section 1.1, *What Makes JRuby So Great?*, on page 2, we discussed some of the deficiencies of this architecture and showed how JRuby can improve it. But the way we ran our application and deployed our code was not very traditional.

With traditional deployment, new versions of an application are released by using a tool like Capistrano or whiskey_disk[6] to pull the code from a repository and push it to a production server. Once the code has been pushed, each application process is restarted. With JRuby, we can reduce the number of processes to one (as we saw in Figure 3, *Architecture of a JRuby web application*, on page 4), which makes it faster to get back online after a deployment.

But the architecture we built in Chapter 3, *Deploying an Archive File*, on page 37 with Warbler and Tomcat greatly impacted the way we deployed code to the server. Instead of pulling code from a repository, we packaged everything into an archive file. Furthermore, we didn't run our application. We dropped the archive file into a container that was already running. There are advantages to this kind of deployment, but it diverges from what traditional Rubyists expect.

Trinidad can help us bridge this gap by providing all the advantages of JRuby with a more traditional framework. We can use it to create an architecture that is similar to the one we set up with Warbler and Tomcat but without creating a WAR. This will complete our picture of traditional deployment on JRuby.

4.2 Getting Started with Trinidad

We don't have to modify Twitalytics at all to start handling web requests with Trinidad. We already prepared it for JRuby in Chapter 1, *Getting Started with JRuby*, on page 1, and Trinidad doesn't require any additional configuration. But we will make changes to the parts of Twitalytics that don't handle web requests, so let's create a new branch based on the jruby branch we started in the aforementioned chapter.

```
$ git checkout -b trinidad jruby
```

---

6.   https://github.com/flogic/whiskey_disk

Next, we'll add trinidad to our Gemfile and run bundle install.

Trinidad/twitalytics/Gemfile
```
gem 'trinidad', '1.3.4'
```

Now we can use the trinidad command to control our server. Let's test it by asking what version is installed.

```
$ trinidad -v
trinidad 1.3.4 (tomcat 7.0.23)
```

This displays both the Trinidad version and the embedded Tomcat version. As we mentioned earlier, Trinidad is a wrapper around the Apache Tomcat container. Tomcat is the same server we used to run our Warbler WAR file in Chapter 3, *Deploying an Archive File*, on page 37, so we've already discussed its many advantages.

Let's boot the server.

```
$ trinidad
Jan 12, 2012 8:25:59 PM org.apache.coyote.AbstractProtocol init
INFO: Initializing ProtocolHandler ["http-bio-3000"]
Jan 12, 2012 8:25:59 PM org.apache.catalina.core.StandardService startInternal
INFO: Starting service Tomcat
Jan 12, 2012 8:25:59 PM org.apache.catalina.core.StandardEngine startInternal
INFO: Starting Servlet Engine: Apache Tomcat/7.0.23
2012-01-13 02:25:59 INFO: No global web.xml found
2012-01-13 02:26:00 INFO: Info: received max runtimes = 5
2012-01-13 02:26:00 INFO: jruby 1.6.7 (ruby-1.8.7-p357) (2012-02-22 3e82bc8)...
2012-01-13 02:26:00 INFO: Info: using runtime pool timeout of 30 seconds
2012-01-13 02:26:00 INFO: Info: received min runtimes = 1
2012-01-13 02:26:00 INFO: Info: received max runtimes = 5
2012-01-13 02:26:11 INFO: Info: add application to the pool. size now = 1
2012-01-13 02:26:11 INFO: Starting ProtocolHandler ["http-bio-3000"]
```

Congratulations. Twitalytics is running on Trinidad. We can see it by pointing our browser to http://localhost:3000.

But let's take a closer look at what was printed to the console when the server was booting. You may have noticed these lines:

```
2012-01-13 02:26:00 INFO: Info: using runtime pool timeout of 30 seconds
2012-01-13 02:26:00 INFO: Info: received min runtimes = 1
2012-01-13 02:26:00 INFO: Info: received max runtimes = 5
2012-01-13 02:26:11 INFO: Info: add application to the pool. size now = 1
```

Trinidad is using a pool of runtimes because our application is not configured to run in thread-safe mode. In Chapter 1, *Getting Started with JRuby*, on page 1, we discussed the implications of this and configured Warbler to use a single runtime instance. Now we'll do the same for Trinidad. Open the config/environments/production.rb file and uncomment this statement:

Trinidad/twitalytics/config/environments/production.rb
```
config.threadsafe!
```

Trinidad is Rails-aware, so this will let it know to use a single instance of our application instead of using a runtime pool, but only in our production environment. For our development environment, we still want to run a single instance to make things start up faster, but we'll configure this by providing the --threadsafe option on the trinidad command. First, kill the currently running Trinidad process by pressing Ctrl+C in that terminal. Then restart it like this:

```
$ trinidad --threadsafe
```

Now when the server is done booting, we'll see this in the console:

```
2012-01-13 02:26:00 INFO: Info: received max runtimes = 1
```

Having one runtime in development helps make start-up time faster. But adding the --threadsafe option every time we run the trinidad command would be cumbersome. Instead, we'll set this in a static configuration file to make it easier.

Let's create a config/trinidad.yml file and add the following attribute to it:

Trinidad/twitalytics/config/trinidad.yml
```
jruby_max_runtimes: 1
```

This will have the same effect as our --threadsafe command-line option.

If the chapter ended here, we'd be right on par with Warbler. But Trinidad has a lot more to offer. Let's move on and add a Trinidad extension that will check our application's compatibility with JRuby every time we start it.

4.3 Adding Trinidad Extensions

Trinidad provides an extension mechanism that allows us to plug in many kinds of features. There are a number of Trinidad extensions that are maintained by the Trinidad developers, but we can also create extensions ourselves. This is particularly useful if we need to hook into the Trinidad life cycle, hook into the application's life cycle, or get a handle to the command-line options the container started up with.

Let's add some extensions to Twitalytics that will improve our infrastructure and development process.

Checking for JRuby Compatibility

Some features of MRI Ruby are not compatible with JRuby. In Chapter 1, *Getting Started with JRuby*, on page 1, we set up the JRuby-Lint tool and ran it manually to inspect Twitalytics for these incompatibilities. But the trinidad_diagnostics_extension extension allows us to run JRuby-Lint inline with our Trinidad application. This will help us keep Twitalytics compatible with JRuby as we continue to develop the application.

To include any Trinidad extension, we start by adding its gem as a dependency. Let's open our Gemfile and add the following statement to it:

Trinidad/twitalytics/Gemfile
```
gem 'trinidad_diagnostics_extension'
```

We then install the gem with Bundler.

```
$ bundle install
...
Installing trinidad_diagnostics_extension (0.1.0)
...
Your bundle is complete! Use `bundle show [gemname]` to see where a bundled ...
```

Now we need to configure Trinidad to load the extension. We could do this by providing the command-line option --load diagnostics. But we'll put this option in our configuration file because we want it to run every time.

Let's open the config/trinidad.yml file we created earlier and add the following attributes to it (be sure to put a line break after the last line):

Trinidad/twitalytics/config/trinidad.yml
```
extensions:
  diagnostics:
```

The previous entry tells Trinidad to load the Diagnostics extension. All Trinidad extensions are named in the form trinidad_<name>_extension. So, loading an extension requires only specifying the <name> part.

Now our server will validate Twitalytics' compatibility with JRuby every time we run the trinidad command. It won't find anything at first, because we already fixed the incompatibilities in Chapter 1, *Getting Started with JRuby*, on page 1. But we can test it by sneaking an Easter egg into our code. Add this statement anywhere in the app/controllers/company_controller.rb file:

```
Kernel.fork {puts "Forking!"}
```

Now let's shut down the server with Ctrl+C and start it up again like this:

```
$ trinidad
...
INFO: Starting Servlet Engine: Apache Tomcat/7.0.23
./app/controllers/company_controller.rb:8: [fork, error] Kernel#fork is not ...
...
2011-11-11 14:45:01 INFO: Starting ProtocolHandler ["http-bio-3000"]
```

Trinidad caught our incompatibility. Now, be sure to remove the fork() call! Rails will reload the controller, so there is no need to restart. The next time we boot the server, the diagnostic extension won't find any problems with our code.

That's all there is to loading a Trinidad extension. In the next section, we'll add an extension that does more than inspect our code; it will run it.

Scheduling Recurring Jobs

As we've eluded to in previous chapters, Twitalytics has some background jobs, and one of them runs at recurring intervals. With MRI, we had to run it in a separate process. But with JRuby and the trinidad_scheduler_extension, we can run it in the same process as the rest of our application without locking up the runtime.

The Scheduler extension allows us to schedule background jobs for execution at a recurring intervals. This allows it to replace tools like crontab[7] or Whenever.[8] But unlike those other tools, it runs in the same process as our application.

At the core of this extension is the very powerful Java-based Quartz Scheduler.[9] But we'll be able to adapt our existing scheduled job to this Java framework with pure Ruby. Before we do that, let's explain what the job does.

Twitalytics collects public tweets that reference a company or product and then provides reports based on its analysis of trends in those tweets. You can see this feature by following the Customers link on the Twitalytics dashboard, which will open the web page illustrated in Figure 10, *The Customers page of Twitalytics*, on page 63.

For Twitalytics to do its analysis, it must store the tweets in the database. Thus, it creates a Status object for each tweet in the feed. In this way, it avoids having to pull the tweets from Twitter for every report and to keep them all in memory.

---

7. http://pubs.opengroup.org/onlinepubs/9699919799/utilities/crontab.html
8. https://github.com/javan/whenever
9. http://quartz-scheduler.org/

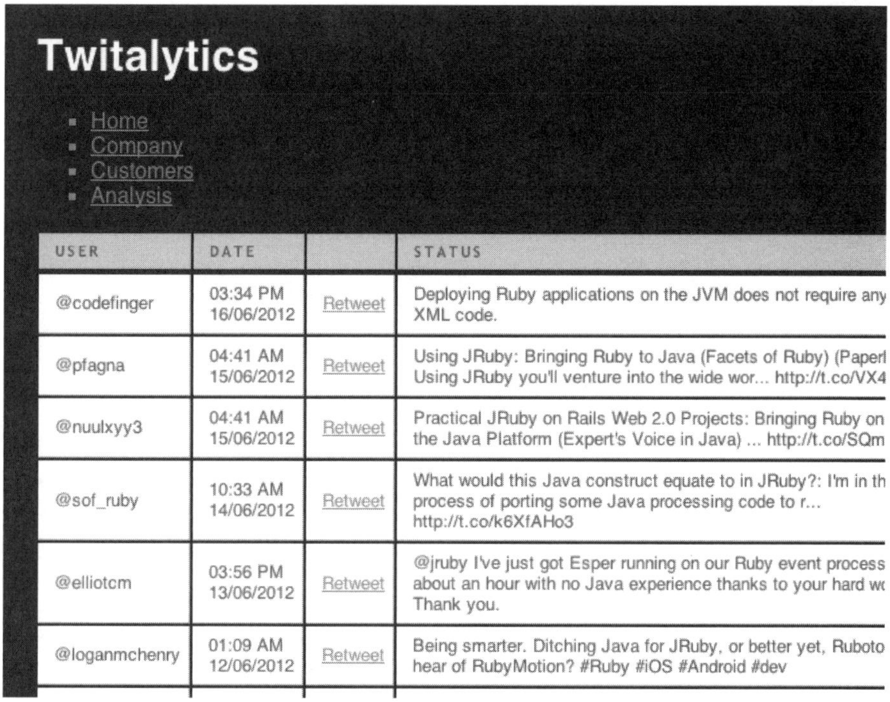

Figure 10—The Customers page of Twitalytics

Unfortunately, creating a new database record for each tweet will cause the database to grow very quickly, especially if the company or product is popular. That is why Twitalytics has a scheduled job that deletes Status records more than thirty days old. The application runs its analytics only against recent tweets, so removing these old statuses won't degrade its reports.

The cleanup job is located in the lib/jobs/delete_old_statuses.rb file, and it looks like this:

twitalytics/lib/jobs/delete_old_statuses.rb

```
class DeleteOldStatuses
  def run
    ids = Status.where("created_at < ?", 30.days.ago)
    if ids.size > 0
      Status.destroy(ids)
      puts "#{ids.size} statuses have been deleted!"
    else
      puts "No statuses have been deleted."
    end
  end
end
DeleteOldStatuses.new.run
```

We can test the earlier script by using the rails runner command. But first, we need to shut down our Trinidad server if it's still running and clean out our development database by running these commands:

```
$ rake db:drop
$ rake db:migrate
```

Now we can test the job by running this:

```
$ rails runner lib/jobs/delete_old_statuses.rb
No statuses have been deleted.
```

No Status records were deleted this time because we haven't persisted any yet. We'll get to that in a moment.

When Twitalytics was running on MRI, this background job was scheduled by adding a crontab entry and having the cron daemon run the previous command. But this increased the complexity of our infrastructure (since cron became another dependency) and made it less portable (it didn't work on Windows).

Fortunately, we can simplify the infrastructure required to run this job. First, let's add the trinidad_scheduler_extension gem to our Gemfile below the other Trinidad dependencies and run bundle install.

Trinidad/twitalytics/Gemfile
```
gem 'trinidad_scheduler_extension'
```

Next, we need to add the scheduler extension to the Trinidad configuration. Open the config/trinidad.yml file and add the scheduler: attribute thusly:

Trinidad/twitalytics/config/trinidad.yml
```
extensions:
  diagnostics:
  scheduler:
```

Now we can modify the delete_old_statuses.rb file to fit the new scheduler's expectations. First remove this line from the end of the script:

twitalytics/lib/jobs/delete_old_statuses.rb
```
DeleteOldStatuses.new.run
```

This statement was instantiating a new DeleteOldStatuses object and calling its run() method. We no longer need it because the Trinidad scheduler will execute those steps as necessary.

We also need to modify the class definition so that DeleteOldStatuses gets registered with the scheduler.

Trinidad/twitalytics/lib/jobs/delete_old_statuses.rb
```
class DeleteOldStatuses < TrinidadScheduler.Cron "0 0/5 * * * ?"
```

The TrinidadScheduler.Cron method takes a cron expression as an argument and returns an anonymous class that our job extends. The anonymous class knows how to register our job with the scheduler. The cron expression we provided schedules the job to run every five minutes (if you don't feel like waiting that long, you can change it to something like *0 * * * * ?*, which will cause it to run every minute).

The next change we'll make to the DeleteOldStatuses class involves the ActiveRecord connection. We have to ensure that it is returned to the pool. When the job ran on MRI, it ran in its own process and had its own connection pool, which disappeared at the end of the job. The pool was really a false pool.

But the trinidad_scheduler_extension instantiates our class once and keeps it around for the life of the application. This allows the connection pool to live beyond each run of the job.

We can ensure that the connection is returned to the pool by wrapping our run() method in a with_connection() block as follows:

Trinidad/twitalytics/lib/jobs/delete_old_statuses.rb
```
def run
  ActiveRecord::Base.connection_pool.with_connection do
    ids = Status.where("created_at < ?", 30.days.ago)

    if ids.size > 0
      Status.destroy(ids)
      puts "#{ids.size} statuses have been deleted!"
    else
      puts "No statuses have been deleted."
    end
  end
end
```

The last step is to load the job into the application. The cron daemon used rails runner to execute the script explicitly. But we'll have to load the script file into Rails with an initializer. Let's create a config/initializers/jobs.rb file and add this code to it:

Trinidad/twitalytics/config/initializers/jobs.rb
```
if $servlet_context
  require 'lib/jobs/delete_old_statuses.rb'
end
```

Anatomy of a cron Expression

The cron tool is a job-scheduling program that is available on most Unix and Linux operating systems. The technologies in this book don't use cron directly, but they rely on cron expressions for their job configuration.

A cron expression is a string composed of seven fields separated by whitespace. Each field can contain any of the allowed values, along with certain combinations of special characters. The seven fields and their allowed values are as follows:

Seconds	Minutes	Hours	Day of Month	Month	Day of Week	Year
0-59	0-59	0-23	1-31	1-12 or JAN-DEC	1-7 or SUN-SAT	1970-2099 (optional)

A few of the special characters include the following:

* The asterisk is used to select all values within a field. For example, * in the Minute field means *every minute*.

? The question mark represents no specific value. For example, if we want a job to fire on a particular day of the month but don't care what day of the week that happens to be, we can put *10* in the Day of Month field and put *?* in the Day of Week field.

/ The forward slash is used to specific increments. For example, *0/15* in the Seconds field means *the seconds 0, 15, 30, and 45*.

- The dash is used to specific ranges. For example, *4-6* in the Hours field means *the hours 4, 5 and 6*.

, The comma is used to specific multiple values. For example, *MON,FRI* in the Day of Week field means *Monday and Friday*.

A cron expression can be as simple as the following string, which schedules a job to run once a year on midnight of January 1:

```
0 0 1 1 * ?
```

Or it can be more complex like this one, which schedules a job to run at 2:10 p.m. and 2:44 p.m. every Monday through Friday in March:

```
0 10,44 14 ? 3 MON-FRI ?
```

cron expressions can be confusing, but they are very powerful. In addition, the cron tool has been around for such a long time that this expression language has proven itself to be very effective.

The guard clause prevents the job from being loaded if Rails is running outside of the Trinidad server. Without this, commands like rails console and rake db:migrate would not work.[10]

---

10. https://github.com/trinidad/trinidad_scheduler_extension/issues/2

Now we can test the job by creating a dummy Status record that is ready to be deleted. We'll use the rails console command to execute the following statement:

```
Status.create(:status_text => 'test',
              :creator => 'tester',
              :created_at => 31.days.ago)
```

The complete command will look like this:

```
$ rails console
Loading development environment (Rails 3.2.1)
jruby-1.6.7 :001 > Status.create(:status_text => 'test',
jruby-1.6.7 :002 >      :creator => 'tester',
jruby-1.6.7 :003 >      :created_at => 31.days.ago)
  SQL (1.0ms)  INSERT INTO "statuses" ("created_at", "creator", "followers_coun
t", "positivity_score", "remote_id", "status_text", "updated_at") VALUES ('20
12-01-15 23:23:32.502000', 'tester', NULL, NULL, NULL, 'test', '2012-02-15 23
:23:32.874000')
 => #<Status id: 23, status_text: "test", creator: "tester", remote_id: nil, fo
llowers_count: nil, positivity_score: nil, created_at: "2012-01-15 23:23:32",
updated_at: "2012-02-15 23:23:32">
```

Good. Let's terminate rails console with the exit statement, which will return us to the command prompt. Now we can run the application and watch the console output for a message from our job.

```
$ trinidad
Feb 15, 2012 5:12:49 PM org.apache.coyote.AbstractProtocol init
INFO: Initializing ProtocolHandler ["http-bio-3000"]
Feb 15, 2012 5:12:49 PM org.apache.catalina.core.StandardService startInte...
INFO: Starting service Tomcat
Feb 15, 2012 5:12:49 PM org.apache.catalina.core.StandardEngine startInternal
INFO: Starting Servlet Engine: Apache Tomcat/7.0.23
2012-02-15 23:12:50 INFO: No global web.xml found
2012-02-15 17:12:52,122 INFO [pool-2-thread-1] ApplicationContext - Info: ...
2012-02-15 17:12:52,130 INFO [pool-2-thread-1] ApplicationContext - jruby ...
2012-02-15 17:13:00,199 INFO [pool-2-thread-1] SimpleThreadPool - Job exec...
2012-02-15 17:13:00,225 INFO [pool-2-thread-1] SchedulerSignalerImpl - Ini...
2012-02-15 17:13:00,227 INFO [pool-2-thread-1] QuartzScheduler - Quartz Sc...
2012-02-15 17:13:00,230 INFO [pool-2-thread-1] RAMJobStore - RAMJobStore i...
2012-02-15 17:13:00,232 INFO [pool-2-thread-1] QuartzScheduler - Scheduler...
  Scheduler class: 'org.quartz.core.QuartzScheduler' - running locally.
  NOT STARTED.
  Currently in standby mode.
  Number of jobs executed: 0
  Using thread pool 'org.quartz.simpl.SimpleThreadPool' - with 10 threads.
  Using job-store 'org.quartz.simpl.RAMJobStore' - which does not support ...

2012-02-15 17:13:00,232 INFO [pool-2-thread-1] StdSchedulerFactory - Quart...
2012-02-15 17:13:00,233 INFO [pool-2-thread-1] StdSchedulerFactory - Quart...
2012-02-15 17:13:00,239 INFO [pool-2-thread-1] QuartzScheduler - JobFactor...
```

```
2012-02-15 17:13:01,248 INFO [pool-2-thread-1] QuartzScheduler - Scheduler...
2012-02-15 23:13:01 INFO: Starting ProtocolHandler ["http-bio-3000"]
2012-02-15 17:13:03,599 INFO [Timer-0] UpdateChecker - New Quartz update(s...
```

This output tells us that the scheduler has started a thread pool that it will use to run our jobs. After a few minutes, we'll see this output:

```
2012-02-15 17:37:01,355 INFO [Quartz::Default::Application_Worker-1] Applicat
ionContext -    (1.0ms)  SELECT COUNT(*) FROM "statuses" WHERE (created_at <
'2012-01-16 23:37:01.266000')

2012-02-15 17:37:01,361 INFO [Quartz::Default::Application_Worker-1] Applicat
ionContext -   Status Load (1.0ms)  SELECT "statuses".* FROM "statuses" WHERE
 (created_at < '2012-01-16 23:37:01.266000')

2012-02-15 17:37:01,416 INFO [Quartz::Default::Application_Worker-1] Applicat
ionContext -   Status Load (0.0ms)  SELECT "statuses".* FROM "statuses" WHERE
 "statuses"."id" = 2 LIMIT 1

2012-02-15 17:37:01,425 INFO [Quartz::Default::Application_Worker-1] Applicat
ionContext -   SQL (0.0ms)  DELETE FROM "statuses" WHERE "statuses"."id" = 2
```

```
1 statuses have been deleted!
```

This means the scheduler has run the job and found our dummy Status instance. A few minutes later, we should see this message again:

```
No statuses have been deleted.
```

Our scheduled job is working.

By using the trinidad_scheduler_extension to run our database-cleaning job instead of cron, we've simplified our production and development infrastructures. We've also made our solution more portable because it now works on Windows.

Next, we need to integrate the background jobs that cannot be scheduled. For example, jobs that run as the result of an external action or user action need to be queued up for processing as the actions occur. Let's use a message queue to do this.

Running Background Jobs with Resque

The next extension we'll add to Twitalytics is the trinidad_resque_extension, which will seamlessly integrate Resque[11] into our application. It will also simplify our infrastructure by running Resque workers as threads inside of our JRuby runtime instead of separate processes.

---

11. https://github.com/defunkt/resque

Resque is a Ruby library for creating background tasks and placing them on a message queue so they can be executed at a later time. We then start a number *workers*, which pull jobs off the queue and process them. With MRI, these workers have to run in their own process, but with Trinidad they can run in separate threads of a JRuby runtime. There are some good resources on the Web if you want to learn more about Resque.[12]

Twitalytics already uses Resque, so we have some task scripts in the lib/workers directory. But we won't have to modify them at all. We only need to add them to our Trinidad configuration.

But first, we need to install Redis[13] on our development machine. Redis is the persistent storage mechanism behind Resque. To install it on Unix and Linux environments, we can run the following commands:

```
$ curl -O redis.googlecode.com/files/redis-2.4.2.tar.gz
$ tar xzf redis-2.4.2.tar.gz
$ cd redis-2.4.2
$ make
```

Redis can't be run on Windows in its native form, but if that's your OS, you can run Redis on the base-jruby virtual machine we created in Chapter 2, *Creating a Deployment Environment*, on page 19. Log into the box with the vagrant ssh command, and run the previous commands. Then map port 6379 on the virtual machine to port 6379 on the host with the config.vm.forward_port(guest_port, host_port) method in our Vagrantfile file. In Chapter 6, *Creating a TorqueBox Application*, on page 103, you'll learn about an even more powerful message queue that TorqueBox provides for us. Unlike Resque and Redis, it's Java-based, so it works on Windows.

After the Redis install completes, the binaries will be available in the src directory of the Redis installation root. We can run the Redis server with this command:

```
$ src/redis-server
[6113] 08 Dec 14:56:07 # Warning: no config file specified, using the ...
[6113] 08 Dec 14:56:07 * Server started, Redis version 2.2.12
[6113] 08 Dec 14:56:07 * The server is now ready to accept connection ...
[6113] 08 Dec 14:56:07 - 0 clients connected (0 slaves), 922160 bytes ...
```

Good. We'll leave Redis running for the duration of the chapter and use it as we test Resque. Next, we need to add the trinidad_resque_extension gem to our Gemfile and run bundle install.

---

12. https://github.com/blog/542-introducing-resque
13. http://redis.io/

Using Resque to Integrate C Extensions

Having Resque and Redis available to our JRuby application gives us an excellent integration point for bringing an MRI Ruby process back into our architecture. A good use case for doing this is the need to add Ruby-based C extensions to an application. For example, you may need RMagick[a] to interface with the ImageMagick[b] and GraphicsMagick[c] image-processing libraries.

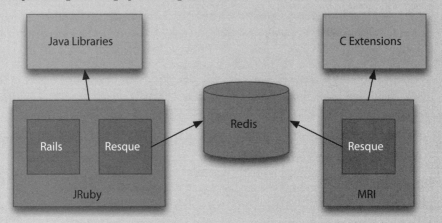

The figure illustrates how this architecture might look. If we need some image processing done, we can queue up jobs from the JRuby process and have our MRI-based Resque workers pull from that queue.

---

a. http://rmagick.rubyforge.org/
b. http://www.imagemagick.org/script/index.php
c. http://www.graphicsmagick.org/

Trinidad/twitalytics/Gemfile
```
gem 'trinidad_resque_extension'
```

Next, we open the config/trinidad.yml file and add a resque: attribute along with our other extensions. But this time, we need to provide configuration options.

Trinidad/twitalytics/config/trinidad.yml
```
extensions:
  diagnostics:
  scheduler:
  resque:
    queues: critical, normal, low
    count:  1
    path: 'lib/workers'
    redis_host: 'localhost:6379'
    work_dir: 'work/resque'
```

First, we specify the queues that our workers will pull jobs from. Next, we set the number of workers that we'll run and the location of our worker jobs. Then, we specify the hostname and port for the Redis server we started earlier. Finally, we define the working directory that Trinidad will use for the Resque log files.

Next, let's enable one of our Resque jobs. We left them disabled in the previous chapters because we were not yet running Redis on our development machine. Now that Redis is running, we need to uncomment the following statement in the find_or_create_from(tweets) method of the app/models/status.rb file:

Trinidad/twitalytics/app/models/status.rb
```
Resque.enqueue(UpdateAnalytics, r.map(&:id))
```

This statement will enqueue a Resque job each time a set of new Status records are created from a Twitter feed. The job that gets enqueued is defined in the lib/workers/update_analytics.rb file.

Now we can test it. Start Twitalytics with the trinidad command, and point a browser to http://localhost:3000/resque. You will see Figure 11, *The Resque overview console*, on page 72. The extension has started both the Resque workers and the console for us. Because of a bug, the Trinidad server may fail to shut down with the Ctrl+C keystroke if it cannot connect to the Redis server.[14] If that happens, we'll have to kill the process with kill -9, Windows Task Manager, or some other platform-specific mechanism.

Now we'll follow the Stats tab in the console, and we'll see that no jobs have been processed and no jobs are pending.

Let's enqueue a Resque job by browsing to the Customers page at http://localhost:3000/customers/index. This will pull new tweets from the customers feed and persist them, which will cause the Resque job to be enqueued.

After the Customers page has loaded, let's return to the Stats page on the Resque console. It should now show that one job has been processed (Figure 12, *The Resque console's Statistics page*, on page 72), and that number should increase each time you reload the Customers page.

Our background job is working! Before we move on, let's commit our changes to the Git repository by running these commands:

```
$ git add .
$ git commit -m "Ported to Trinidad"
```

---

14. https://github.com/trinidad/trinidad_resque_extension/issues/3

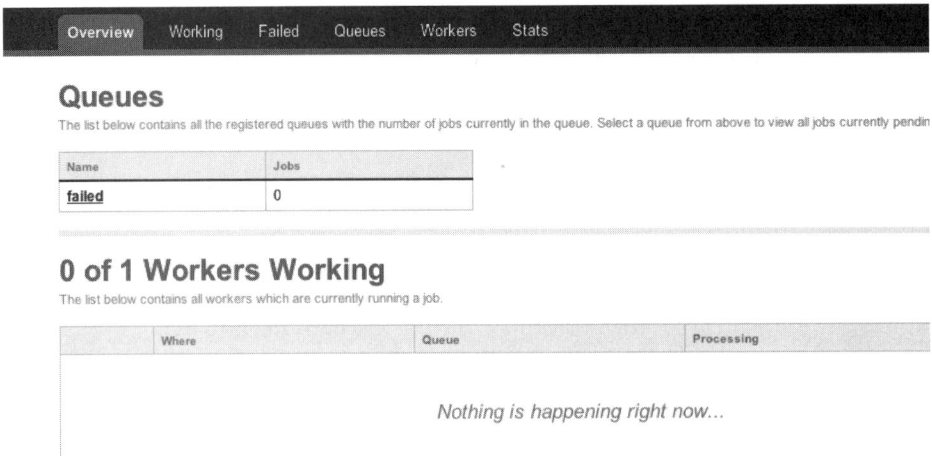

Figure 11—The Resque overview console

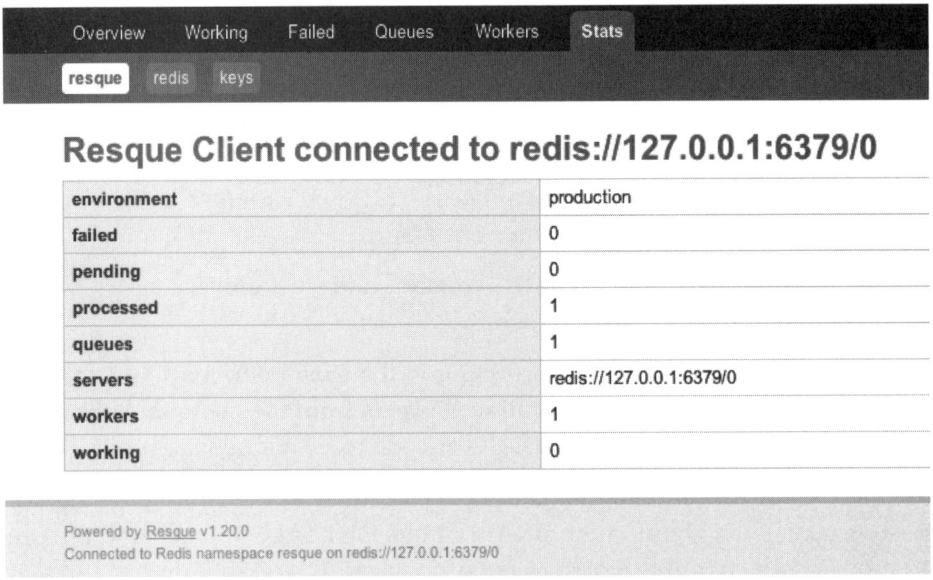

Figure 12—The Resque console's Statistics page

We now have our web server, schedule jobs, and message queue broker all running in the same JRuby process. Trinidad has helped us in making this happen, but it's important to be aware of other solutions that can help facilitate a traditional deployment. We'll discuss a few of them in a moment. But first, we'll take a quick look at a few more extensions.

Exploring Some Other Extensions

There are many Trinidad extensions other than the ones we've already used. A complete list can be found under the Trinidad organization on GitHub.[15] The following is an overview of a few useful ones:

Database connection pooling extension

> One of the disadvantages of having multiple processes in a traditional MRI deployment is that each process has its own connection pool. As you create new processes, you create new pools. As a result, the number of connections is bound to the number of processes and not the size of the pool. Most deployment environments solve this problem by running some kind of middleware that sits between the database and its clients, such as pgpool for PostgreSQL.[16] But this kind of solution further complicates your infrastructure. That's why Trinidad provides a database connection pool that can be shared not only between instances of your application but also by other applications in the container.

Life-cycle extension

> This extension allows you to add life-cycle listeners written in Ruby to the Trinidad's server context as well as each application context that runs on top of Trinidad. It will also allow us to enable the Java Management Extensions (JMX) monitoring capabilities of Tomcat, which we'll discuss in Chapter 9, *Managing a JRuby Deployment*, on page 163.

Sandbox extension

> Having an entire application run in a single process means that you can use a centralized tool to manage and monitor it. The Trinidad sandbox extension provides access to your application through a management console and a REST API. It even runs in the same process as your application, so it won't further complicate your infrastructure.

In Chapter 5, *Deploying a Trinidad Application*, on page 75, we'll add the sandbox extension to our production application. But we've added all the extensions we need for development purposes, so let's move on.

4.4 Choosing Alternatives to Trinidad

Trinidad is one of the best supported platforms for the deployment of JRuby web applications. It's also one of the few commercially supported JRuby web

---

15. https://github.com/trinidad
16. http://pgpool.projects.postgresql.org/

frameworks (via Engine Yard).[17] There are other options for traditional deployment of your JRuby web applications, but none has emerged as a direct competitor to Trinidad. The most promising appears to be Kirk.[18]

Kirk provides a pure Ruby layer on top of the Jetty web server.[19] This is similar to the way Trinidad wraps Tomcat. Kirk gives you all the same advantages of concurrency, garbage collection, and more. But it also provides a mechanism for zero-downtime deploys, which means you can deploy new versions of your application without missing a single request.

If you run a quick Google search for *JRuby web servers*, you will likely find the GlassFish gem. This project was initially backed by Sun Microsystems but was abandoned after its acquisition by Oracle in early 2010. If you decide to use this gem, be aware that it is not moving forward.

In Chapter 6, *Creating a TorqueBox Application*, on page 103, we'll discuss TorqueBox, a framework that can be used for traditional deployment. But it is a more comprehensive solution that could increase the complexity of your deployments. The increase in complexity may be tolerable only when you are using the platform's advanced features.

4.5   Wrapping Up

This chapter has provided an overview of Trinidad's capabilities. But it has also introduced you to how we can make use of the JVM in general. Incorporating the scheduled jobs and message broker into our application has reduced the complexity of our infrastructure by handling web requests, recurring jobs, and background jobs with a single process.

You've learned more than just how to use Trinidad. You've learned how to adapt your thinking to the JVM. This skill will be important as we continue to deploy, monitor, and manage Twitalytics. You'll have a better understanding of what's under the hood, which will help you diagnosis problems.

In the next chapter on page 75, we'll deploy Trinidad and Twitalytics to a production server.

---

17. http://www.engineyard.com/
18. https://github.com/strobecorp/kirk
19. http://jetty.codehaus.org/jetty/

CHAPTER 5

Deploying a Trinidad Application

Deploying an application on JRuby doesn't mean that we have to change our tools and processes. In this chapter, we'll be using familiar technologies such as Capistrano and Git to deploy our code. We'll also run and configure Trinidad in a way that is similar to traditional Ruby web servers like Mongrel, Thin, or Unicorn. As a result, our deployment targets will look very similar to MRI-based environments.

The first deployment target we'll use is a dedicated server. We'll base it on the virtual machine we began in Chapter 2, *Creating a Deployment Environment*, on page 19, and then we'll prepare it the same way we would prepare a traditional MRI deployment. Even though this environment will resemble an MRI-based environment, it will make many improvements to the traditional model. We'll use faster protocols that are not available in MRI, and we'll need to keep only a single runtime instance of our application in memory because of the JVM's native threads. We can also hot-deploy our application, which means we won't have to restart the web server each time we deploy a new version and hog our system's resources. These are all ways in which a JRuby deployment improves upon MRI-based deployments.

In this chapter, we'll also use a managed cloud server as a deployment target. This won't require the maintenance and configuration of a dedicated server, but it will be less flexible. Like the dedicated server, the cloud deployment will closely resemble a cloud-based MRI deployment.

Let's begin by provisioning a dedicated server.

5.1 Provisioning a Server

A dedicated server could be rented from a hosting provider, or it could run on a physical device in a server closet. In either case, it's an environment that requires us to be responsible for all configuration from the operating system up to the application.

The advantage of a dedicated server is that we can tailor our infrastructure to suit the application's needs. The disadvantage is that we have to do more work—so much work, in fact, that you may need to hire more people. A system administrator is often required to keep these kinds of environments running.

In this section, we'll create a virtual environment to use as a deployment target for Twitalytics, which we ported to Trinidad in the previous chapter on page 57. Let's move to our twitalytics directory, which contains the Git repository we created in *Preface*, on page xi, and use the vagrant command to add a new box.

```
$ cd ~/code/twitalytics
$ vagrant box add trinidad base-jruby.box
[vagrant] Downloading with Vagrant::Downloaders::File...
[vagrant] Copying box to temporary location...
[vagrant] Extracting box...
[vagrant] Verifying box...
[vagrant] Cleaning up downloaded box...
```

Next, we need to edit the Vagrantfile and adjust the config.vm.box attribute so it points to the newly created trinidad box.

Trinidad/twitalytics/Vagrantfile
```
config.vm.box = "trinidad"
```

We'll also forward Trinidad's default port of 3000 on the guest to port 8888 on the host.

Trinidad/twitalytics/Vagrantfile
```
config.vm.forward_port 3000, 8888
```

Our Vagrantfile is ready. Let's boot the machine before we move on.

```
$ vagrant up
[default] Importing base box 'trinidad'...
...
[default] The guest additions on this VM do not match the install version of
VirtualBox! This may cause things such as forwarded ports, shared
folders, and more to not work properly. If any of those things fail on
this machine, please update the guest additions and repackage the
box.

Guest Additions Version: 4.1.0
VirtualBox Version: 4.1.8
[default] Matching MAC address for NAT networking...
[default] Clearing any previously set forwarded ports...
[default] Forwarding ports...
```

```
[default] -- 22 => 2222 (adapter 1)
[default] -- 80 => 8000 (adapter 1)
[default] -- 3000 => 8888 (adapter 1)
[default] Creating shared folders metadata...
[default] Clearing any previously set network interfaces...
[default] Booting VM...
[default] Waiting for VM to boot. This can take a few minutes.
[default] VM booted and ready for use!
[default] Mounting shared folders...
[default] -- v-root: /vagrant
[default] -- manifests: /tmp/vagrant-puppet/manifests
[default] -- v-pp-m0: /tmp/vagrant-puppet/modules-0
[default] Running provisioner: Vagrant::Provisioners::Puppet...
[default] Running Puppet with /tmp/vagrant-puppet/manifests/site.pp...
stdin: is not a tty
notice: /Stage[main]//Exec[apt-update]/returns: executed successfully
notice: /Stage[main]/Postgres/Exec[psql -c "ALTER USER vagrant WITH PASSWORD...
notice: Finished catalog run in 9.79 seconds
```

Now let's add some new components to our server configuration.

Installing Redis with Puppet

You'll recall that we installed Redis on our development machine in Chapter 4, *Creating a Trinidad Application*, on page 57 so Resque could run our background jobs. Now we must do the same on our production server, but we'll use Puppet instead of running the commands manually.

First, let's create a module directory for Redis.

```
$ mkdir -p puppet/modules/redis/manifests
```

We also need to create an init.pp manifest file in the new directory. Now we'll open the file and add a redis class that installs the redis-server package and starts the redis-server service.

Trinidad/twitalytics/puppet/modules/redis/manifests/init.pp
```
class redis {
  package { "redis-server":
    ensure => present,
  }

  service { "redis-server":
    ensure  => running,
    require => Package["redis-server"],
  }
}
```

Finally, we'll include the new module in our site.pp file.

Trinidad/twitalytics/puppet/manifests/site.pp

```
include redis
```

Excellent. Let's run the provisioning process again.

```
$ vagrant provision
[default] Running provisioner: Vagrant::Provisioners::Puppet...
[default] Running Puppet with /tmp/vagrant-puppet/manifests/site.pp...
stdin: is not a tty
notice: /Stage[main]//Exec[apt-update]/returns: executed successfully
notice: /Stage[main]/Postgres/Exec[psql -c "ALTER USER vagrant WITH PASSWO...
notice: /Stage[main]/Redis/Package[redis-server]/ensure: ensure changed 'p...
notice: /Stage[main]/Redis/Service[redis-server]/ensure: ensure changed 's...
notice: Finished catalog run in 6.56 seconds
```

Redis is ready! Now we can add Trinidad to our configuration.

5.2 Installing Trinidad as a Service

On our development machine, we installed the Trinidad gem and used the trinidad command to start the server. But that's not how we want to run Trinidad on our production server. Instead, we want Trinidad to run as a service that is controlled by the operating system's init daemon. Fortunately, the trinidad_init_services gem can do this for us, even on Windows.

To use the trinidad_init_services gem, we'll need to install it on our production server and run the configuration script it provides for us. We'll do this with Puppet so the setup becomes part of the portable, reproducible infrastructure scripts we began in Chapter 2, *Creating a Deployment Environment*, on page 19.

Let's start by creating a Puppet module for Trinidad.

```
$ mkdir -p puppet/modules/trinidad/manifests
```

We also need to create an init.pp manifest file to the new directory. Now we'll open this file and add a trinidad class. Inside the class, we'll define a few variables.

Trinidad/twitalytics/puppet/modules/trinidad/manifests/init.pp

```
class trinidad {
  $jruby_home = "/opt/jruby"
  $trinidad_home = "/opt/trinidad"
}
```

The $jruby_home variable references the location of the JRuby runtime we installed in Chapter 2, *Creating a Deployment Environment*, on page 19. The $trinidad_home variable references the location where we'll put our application.

Next, we need to add a resource that installs the trinidad_init_services gem's only native dependency. Add the following configuration immediately after the variables in the trinidad class:

Trinidad/twitalytics/puppet/modules/trinidad/manifests/init.pp
```
package { jsvc :
  ensure => present
}
```

The Java Service (JSVC) package contains a set of libraries that allow Java applications to run more naturally on Unix and Linux systems. The trinidad_init_services gem includes this library (and even a port for Windows), but its version is not compatible with the version of Ubuntu we're running. That's why we are installing it ourselves.

Now we're ready to install the trinidad gem. Let's add the following resource to our class:

Trinidad/twitalytics/puppet/modules/trinidad/manifests/init.pp
```
exec {  install_trinidad :
  command => "jruby -S gem install trinidad -v 1.3.4",
  path    => "${jruby_home}/bin:${path}",
  creates => "${jruby_home}/bin/trinidad",
  require => File[$jruby_home]
}
```

This resource adds the ${jruby_home}/bin directory to the path and runs the gem install command. It also declares that this resource creates a ${jruby_home}/bin/trinidad file, so it won't run if that file already exists.

Now we can install the trinidad_init_services gem by adding this resource to our class.

Trinidad/twitalytics/puppet/modules/trinidad/manifests/init.pp
```
exec {  install_trinidad_init_services :
  command => "jruby -S gem install trinidad_init_services -v 1.1.3",
  path    => "${jruby_home}/bin:${path}",
  creates => "${jruby_home}/bin/trinidad_init_service",
  require => [Package[jsvc], Exec[install_trinidad], File[$jruby_home]]
}
```

This installs the trinidad_init_services gem in the same way the previous resource installed Trinidad. It also defines explicit dependencies on the jsvc, install_trinidad, and $jruby_home resources. Puppet manifests are declarative, so the order of resources in a file doesn't guarantee execution order by default. One way to guarantee that a given resource executes before another is with the require attribute.

This is a good point to save our init.pp file and test things. But first, we need to include the Trinidad module in our puppet/manifest/site.pp manifest. Open it, and add this line:

Trinidad/twitalytics/puppet/manifests/site.pp
```
include trinidad
```

Now we can provision the box.

```
$ vagrant provision
[default] Running provisioner: Vagrant::Provisioners::Puppet...
[default] Running Puppet with /tmp/vagrant-puppet/manifests/site.pp...
stdin: is not a tty
notice: /Stage[main]//Exec[apt-update]/returns: executed successfully
notice: /Stage[main]/Postgres/Exec[psql -c "ALTER USER vagrant WITH PASSWORD...
notice: /Stage[main]/Trinidad/Package[jsvc]/ensure: ensure changed 'purged' ...
notice: /Stage[main]/Redis/Service[redis-server]/ensure: ensure changed 'sto...
notice: /Stage[main]/Trinidad/Exec[install_trinidad]/returns: executed succe...
notice: /Stage[main]/Trinidad/Exec[install_trinidad_init_services]/returns: ...
notice: Finished catalog run in 17.87 seconds
```

Great. We've created our application directory and installed JSVC, and most importantly we've installed the trinidad_init_services gem. But before we can use the gem, we need to create a configuration file that's specific to our environment. We can do this by creating a Puppet template file.

Let's add a templates directory to our module, which will contain our template file.

```
$ mkdir -p puppet/modules/trinidad/templates/
```

Now we need to create a trinidad_config.yml.erb file in this new directory. We've named it this way because when the template is turned into a real file on the production server, it will be called trinidad_config.yml. We've added the .erb extension because Puppet will run our template through ERb. That will allow us to use the $jruby_home and $trinidad_path variables.

Let's edit the trinidad_config.yml.erb file and add the following code to it:

Trinidad/twitalytics/puppet/modules/trinidad/templates/trinidad_config.yml.erb
```
app_path: "<%= trinidad_home %>/current"
trinidad_options: "-e production"
jruby_home: "<%= jruby_home %>"
ruby_compat_version: RUBY1_8
trinidad_name: Trinidad
jsvc_path: "/usr/bin/jsvc"
java_home: "/usr/lib/jvm/java-6-openjdk/jre"
output_path: "/etc/init.d"
pid_file: "<%= trinidad_home %>/shared/pids/trinidad.pid"
log_file: "<%= trinidad_home %>/shared/log/trinidad.log"
```

Most of the previous configuration options are boilerplate. But notice that we've used ERb tags to inject the variables. We've also specified the path to the JSVC executable, our Java home directory, and the location of our init.d directory.

Now we need to create a resource that will process our template into a real file. Open the init.pp file, and add this element to its class:

Trinidad/twitalytics/puppet/modules/trinidad/manifests/init.pp
```
file { "${trinidad_home}/trinidad_config.yml":
  content => template("trinidad/trinidad_config.yml.erb"),
  require => Exec[install_trinidad_init_services]
}
```

Now we'll add a resource that creates the service by passing this file to the trinidad_init_service command, which is provided by the trinidad_init_services gem. Open the init.pp file, and add this code:

Trinidad/twitalytics/puppet/modules/trinidad/manifests/init.pp
```
exec { trinidad_init_service :
  command => "jruby -S trinidad_init_service ${trinidad_home}/trinidad_config.yml",
  path    => "${jruby_home}/bin:${path}",
  creates => "/etc/init.d/trinidad",
  require => File["${trinidad_home}/trinidad_config.yml", $jruby_home]
}
```

This resource runs the trinidad_init_service command with the trinidad_config.yml file. It also defines that it will create a /etc/init.d/trinidad file, so it won't run if that file already exists.

Next, we need to add a couple of resources that adjust the access rights of the files created by the trinidad_init_service command. Add this code to the class:

Trinidad/twitalytics/puppet/modules/trinidad/manifests/init.pp
```
file { "${trinidad_home}/shared" :
  owner => vagrant,
  ensure => directory,
  recurse => true,
  require => Exec[trinidad_init_service]
}

file { "/etc/init.d/trinidad" :
  owner => "vagrant",
  require => Exec[trinidad_init_service]
}
```

The first resource changes the owner of the $trinidad_home/shared directory to the vagrant user. The second resource does the same for our init.d script, so our vagrant user can run the script.

Finally, we need to run the provisioning process again.

```
$ vagrant provision
[default] Running provisioner: Vagrant::Provisioners::Puppet...
[default] Running Puppet with /tmp/vagrant-puppet/manifests/site.pp...
stdin: is not a tty
notice: /Stage[main]//Exec[apt-update]/returns: executed successfully
notice: /Stage[main]/Postgres/Exec[psql -c "ALTER USER vagrant WITH PASSWORD...
notice: /Stage[main]/Redis/Service[redis-server]/ensure: ensure changed 'sto...
notice: /Stage[main]/Trinidad/File[/opt/trinidad/trinidad_config.yml]/ensure...
notice: /Stage[main]/Trinidad/Exec[trinidad_init_service]/returns: executed ...
notice: /Stage[main]/Trinidad/File[/etc/init.d/trinidad]/owner: owner change...
notice: /File[/opt/trinidad/shared]/owner: owner changed 'root' to 'vagrant'
notice: /File[/opt/trinidad/shared/log]/owner: owner changed 'root' to 'vagr...
notice: /File[/opt/trinidad/shared/pids]/owner: owner changed 'root' to 'vag...
notice: Finished catalog run in 6.61 seconds
```

We've successfully installed Trinidad as a service! But the service isn't running. We'll leave that to Capistrano.

5.3 Hot-Deploying with Capistrano

Capistrano is a tool for running commands and scripts on remote servers, which makes it an excellent tool for deploying code from one machine to another. In the earlier chapters, we eliminated the need for Capistrano by using Warbler to create an archive file, but that may not work for every organization. If your team is already familiar with Capistrano, then there may not be a need to change. Furthermore, Trinidad works well with Capistrano because it is designed to behave like a traditional Ruby web server.

We'll be deploying from our development environment to our virtual production server, but we could deploy from one remote server to another or one Git repository to a remote server. The deployment pattern you should use in the real world depends on your organization and the processes that drive a release.

We're going to use Capistrano to hot-deploy Twitalytics. This means that once Trinidad is running, we can boot new versions of our application without restarting the web server. As a result, each deployment will require fewer resources, and the application can start serving requests quicker.

Let's deploy our application to Trinidad. We're going to create a custom Capistrano recipe, which is a script that tells Capistrano how to push our code.

Creating a Deployment Recipe

We'll start by adding Capistrano to our dependencies. Open the Twitalytics Gemfile, and add the following code to the end of it:

Trinidad/twitalytics/Gemfile
```
gem 'capistrano'
gem 'ffi-ncurses'
```

The first dependency is Capistrano. The second dependency, ffi-ncurses,[1] is a pure-Ruby wrapper for the ncurses tool.[2] JRuby can't use the native C-extensions that MRI relies on, so we often have to include these pure-Ruby dependencies to get things done. But it's not necessarily a bad thing. Using pure-Ruby instead of native code makes our tools more portable.

Before we move on, let's run Bundler.

```
$ bundle install
...
Installing capistrano (2.9.0)
...
Installing ffi-ncurses (0.4.0)
...
Your bundle is complete! Use `bundle show [gemname]` to see where ...
```

Now we need to make our application Capistrano-ready. Run the following command from the Twitalytics root directory:

```
$ capify .
[add] writing './Capfile'
[add] writing './config/deploy.rb'
[done] capified!
```

The capify command created two files for us. The Capfile contains boilerplate code that sets up our root directory for Capistrano. But the config/deploy.rb file contains the code for our recipe. Let's open it and replace its contents with the following statement:

Trinidad/twitalytics/config/deploy.rb
```
require 'bundler/capistrano'
```

This require statement loads Bundler's Capistrano support into our script. This will cause Capistrano to run bundle install on our production server.

Next, we'll configure our server's domain name and tell Capistrano what roles it plays.

---

1. https://github.com/seanohalpin/ffi-ncurses
2. http://invisible-island.net/ncurses/

Trinidad/twitalytics/config/deploy.rb
```
server "localhost", :app, :db, :primary => true
```

The virtual machine we've created will act as both our application server and our database server. We've added those Capistrano roles to it and set it as the primary server.

Now we need to configure how Capistrano will connect to this server. Capistrano uses SSH, and as you'll recall from Chapter 2, *Creating a Deployment Environment*, on page 19, we're using port 2222 with the Vagrant-provided SSH key to connect to our server. Let's tell Capistrano about these connection parameters.

Trinidad/twitalytics/config/deploy.rb
```
ssh_options[:port] = 2222
ssh_options[:keys] = "~/.vagrant.d/insecure_private_key"
```

Great, now Capistrano can connect in the same way as our vagrant ssh command.

We also need to set the username Capistrano will log in as and run our deployment with.

Trinidad/twitalytics/config/deploy.rb
```
set :user, "vagrant"
set :group, "vagrant"
set :use_sudo, false
```

The previous statements tell Capistrano to connect to our virtual machine as the vagrant user and not to use the sudo command as it deploys our code.

Next, we'll configure our application settings. We need to tell Capistrano how and where to deploy Twitalytics.

Trinidad/twitalytics/config/deploy.rb
```
set :deploy_to, "/opt/trinidad"
set :application, "twitalytics"
set :repository, "."
set :scm, :none
set :deploy_via, :copy
set :copy_exclude, [".git","log","tmp","*.box","*.war",".idea",".DS_Store"]
```

The first two statements tell Capistrano the deployment directory and the name of our application. Then, we set the :repository attribute to our root directory and the source control management (SCM) attribute to :none. This configuration is slightly uncharacteristic of most Capistrano deployments, which use Git. But we haven't set up a globally accessible SCM repository, so the deployment we've configured is more typical of a strategy that uses a continuous integration (CI) server to push code updates. A CI server is a tool for continuously building and deploying code, and we'll use one in Chapter 10, *Using a Continuous Integration Server*, on page 181. That's why we've set the :deploy_to attribute to :copy. This will package our source code into a tarball and push it to the server.

Next, we need to configure how Capistrano will run commands on our server.

Trinidad/twitalytics/config/deploy.rb
```
set :default_environment,
  'PATH' => "/opt/jruby/bin:$PATH",
  'JSVC_ARGS_EXTRA' => "-user vagrant"
set :bundle_dir, ""
set :bundle_flags, "--system --quiet"
```

We're adding the JRuby home directory we created in Chapter 2, *Creating a Deployment Environment*, on page 19 to our path. We also set an environment variable that will cause the Trinidad service to run as our vagrant user. Then we tell Bundler not to use its own directory and to install gems to the system instead. By default, Capistrano will tell Bundler to puts its gems in the shared/bundler directory. But in Section 5.2, *Installing Trinidad as a Service*, on page 78, we set up Trinidad to run from our system gem directory. Normally, this wouldn't matter, but because we're using Trinidad extensions, we need the application gems to be on the system gem path.

Now we can set up a few deployment tasks. We'll need to create a :deploy namespace and add a task to install Bundler. We'll also add an instruction to invoke this task before the deploy:setup task, which we'll be using in the next section.

Trinidad/twitalytics/config/deploy.rb
```
before "deploy:setup", "deploy:install_bundler"

namespace :deploy do
  task :install_bundler, :roles => :app do
    run "sudo gem install bundler"
  end
end
```

Next, we need to add a task that tells Capistrano how to start our server using the /etc/init.d/trinidad script that was created in Section 5.2, *Installing Trinidad as a Service*, on page 78. Add the following code to the :deploy namespace block:

Trinidad/twitalytics/config/deploy.rb
```
task :start, :roles => :app do
  run "/etc/init.d/trinidad start"
end
```

We also need to create a :stop task in the same namespace. But this task won't do anything.

Trinidad/twitalytics/config/deploy.rb
```
task :stop, :roles => :app do end
```

This task is empty because we don't want to stop Trinidad. Instead, we want to hot-deploy our application when the :restart task is invoked. To do this, we'll add the following task to the :deploy namespace:

Trinidad/twitalytics/config/deploy.rb
```
task :restart, :roles => :app do
  run "touch #{current_release}/tmp/restart.txt"
end
```

Trinidad supports hot deployment, which means we can update our application code and redeploy without restarting the Trinidad server. It does this by monitoring a tmp/restart.txt file in our application directory. When the monitored file is modified, Trinidad redeploys the application. This is illustrated by the two phases in Figure 13, *Trinidad hot deployment*, on page 87. Hot deployment is a huge improvement over traditional Ruby servers because it reduces the time and resources required to deploy updates.

Great, we're done writing the config/deploy.rb configuration. Now let's deploy Twitalytics.

Running the Deployment Script

The Capistrano gem provides a number of deployment tasks that we can use. Let's get a list of them by running the following command:

```
$ cap -T
cap bundle:install          # Install the current Bundler environment.
cap deploy                  # Deploys your project.
cap deploy:check            # Test deployment dependencies.
cap deploy:cleanup          # Clean up old releases.
cap deploy:cold             # Deploys and starts a `cold' application.
cap deploy:migrate          # Run the migrate rake task.
cap deploy:migrations       # Deploy and run pending migrations.
cap deploy:pending          # Displays the commits since your last deploy.
cap deploy:pending:diff     # Displays the `diff' since your last deploy.
cap deploy:rollback         # Rolls back to a previous version and restarts.
cap deploy:rollback:code    # Rolls back to the previously deployed version.
cap deploy:setup            # Prepares one or more servers for deployment.
cap deploy:symlink          # Updates the symlink to the most recently deployed ...
cap deploy:update           # Copies your project and updates the symlink.
cap deploy:update_code      # Copies your project to the remote servers.
cap deploy:upload           # Copy files to the currently deployed version.
cap deploy:web:disable      # Present a maintenance page to visitors.
```

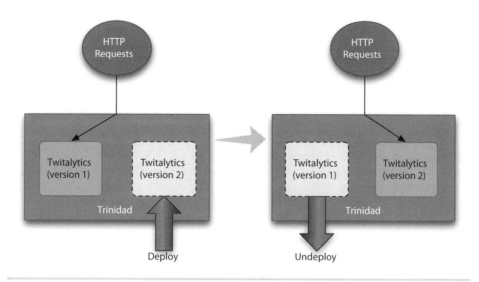

Figure 13—Trinidad hot deployment

```
cap deploy:web:enable    # Makes the application web-accessible again.
cap invoke               # Invoke a single command on the remote servers.
cap shell                # Begin an interactive Capistrano session.
...
```

All of these are useful, especially the invoke task, which we'll be using in a moment. But first we need to prepare our server environment. Let's make sure our the virtual machine is still running by executing this command:

```
$ vagrant status
Current VM states:

default                  running

The VM is running. To stop this VM, you can run `vagrant halt` to
shut it down forcefully, or you can run `vagrant suspend` to simply
suspend the virtual machine. In either case, to restart it again,
simply run `vagrant up`.
```

If the status is different from what is shown here, then boot the server with the vagrant up command. Now we can use the cap deploy:setup task, which prepares our environment.

```
$ cap deploy:setup
  * executing `deploy:setup'
    triggering before callbacks for `deploy:setup'
  * executing `deploy:install_bundler'
  * executing "sudo gem install bundler"
```

```
    servers: ["localhost"]
    [localhost] executing command
 ** [out :: localhost] Successfully installed bundler-1.0.22
 ** [out :: localhost]
 ** [out :: localhost] 1 gem installed
 ** [out :: localhost]
    command finished in 9787ms
  * executing "mkdir -p /opt/trinidad /opt/trinidad/releases /opt/trinidad...
    servers: ["localhost"]
    [localhost] executing command
    command finished in 28ms
  * executing "chmod g+w /opt/trinidad /opt/trinidad/releases /opt/trinida...
    servers: ["localhost"]
    [localhost] executing command
    command finished in 28ms
```

Let's examine the output. As you'll recall from our deployment script, we defined the deploy:install_bundler task to run before the deploy:setup task, so that's the first thing that happens. Next, the task creates the application directories on the server and sets their permissions accordingly. The resulting structure looks like this:

```
/opt/trinidad/
|-- releases/
`-- shared/
  |-- log/
  |-- system/
  `-- pids/
```

The shared directory is where we've configured the Trinidad service to put its log and PID files. The releases directory is where Capistrano will put a copy of our application each time we push new code.

Let's push our first release by running the deploy:cold task. This one command will invoke a number of tasks. It will update our code, which creates a new directory under the releases directory that represents our release. It also creates a current symlink to our release directory. Finally, it migrates our database and starts the Trinidad service.

```
$ cap deploy:cold
  * executing `deploy:cold'
    triggering before callbacks for `deploy:cold'
  * executing `deploy:update'
 ** transaction: start
 ...
 ** transaction: commit
  * executing `deploy:migrate'
  * executing "cd /opt/trinidad/releases/20120216203509 && bundle exec rake...
    servers: ["localhost"]
```

```
   [localhost] executing command
** [out :: localhost] ==  CreateStatuses: migrating ======================...
** [out :: localhost] -- create_table(:statuses)
** [out :: localhost] -> 0.0340s
** [out :: localhost] -> 0 rows
** [out :: localhost] ==  CreateStatuses: migrated (0.0450s) =============...
** [out :: localhost]
** [out :: localhost] ==  CreateAnalytics: migrating ======================...
** [out :: localhost]
** [out :: localhost] -- create_table(:analytics)
** [out :: localhost]
** [out :: localhost] -> 0.0160s
** [out :: localhost]
** [out :: localhost] -> 0 rows
** [out :: localhost]
** [out :: localhost] ==  CreateAnalytics: migrated (0.0190s) ============...
** [out :: localhost]
** [out :: localhost]
   command finished in 30657ms
 * executing `deploy:start'
 * executing "/etc/init.d/trinidad start"
   servers: ["localhost"]
   [localhost] executing command
** [out :: localhost] Starting trinidad daemon...
** [out :: localhost] Daemon exited with status: 1. Check pidfile and log
   command finished in 4070ms
```

Let's check the server's log file by using Capistrano to invoke a remote command.

```
$ cap invoke COMMAND="tail /opt/trinidad/shared/log/trinidad.log"
 * executing `invoke'
 * executing "tail -f /opt/trinidad/shared/log/trinidad.log"
   servers: ["localhost"]
   [localhost] executing command
   [localhost] env PATH=/opt/jruby/bin:$PATH sh -c 'tail -f /opt/trinidad...
** [out :: localhost] Number of jobs executed: 0
** [out :: localhost] Using thread pool 'org.quartz.simpl.SimpleThreadPoo...
** [out :: localhost] Using job-store 'org.quartz.simpl.RAMJobStore' - wh...
** [out :: localhost]
** [out :: localhost] 2012-02-22 08:59:55,813 INFO [pool-2-thread-1] StdS...
** [out :: localhost] 2012-02-22 08:59:55,814 INFO [pool-2-thread-1] StdS...
** [out :: localhost] 2012-02-22 08:59:55,822 INFO [pool-2-thread-1] Quar...
** [out :: localhost] 2012-02-22 08:59:59,156 INFO [pool-2-thread-1] Quar...
** [out :: localhost] 2012-02-22 16:59:59 INFO: Starting ProtocolHandler ...
** [out :: localhost] 2012-02-22 09:00:01,101 INFO [Timer-0] UpdateChecke...
** [out :: localhost] No statuses have been deleted.
   command finished in 187ms
```

We need to run the deploy:cold task only the first time we deploy. For subsequent releases, we can use the deploy task. We can try it by pushing another release.

```
$ cap deploy
* executing `deploy'
...
* executing `deploy:restart'
* executing "touch /opt/trinidad/releases/20111128140150/tmp/...
  servers: ["localhost"]
  [localhost] executing command
  command finished in 27ms
```

We'll be using this command to update the server as we make changes to Twitalytics in this chapter.

Finally, we'll point a browser to http://localhost:8888. Twitalytics is running in production. Now we need to open it up to the world by running Apache in front of it.

5.4 Configuring Apache

Most Ruby deployments use an HTTP server as a proxy for the Ruby servers that handle dynamic content. The HTTP server's job is to handle security, routing, load balancing, and static content. Of these jobs, load balancing is particularly important because a single machine will run multiple application instances. Thus, load balancing is the only means by which parallelism can be achieved in an MRI deployment.

In our JRuby deployment, Trinidad uses a single application instance per machine, which eliminates the need for load balancing on a single machine. But we'll still need an HTTP server for load balancing if we want to use that machine as part of a distributed cluster. We also need an HTTP server to provide support for implementing Secure Sockets Layer (SSL) on top of our HTTP layer. As a result, we'll enhance our deployment architecture by including the Apache HTTP Server as a proxy for the Trinidad server.

The Apache HTTP Server is an extremely mature and well-supported piece of software that is the most popular of its kind.[3] Many Ruby deployments use Apache, but there are numerous others that use alternatives such as Ngnix. We've chosen Apache because it pairs well with the Apache Tomcat server.

Because Trinidad is a wrapper around Tomcat, it gives us access to some powerful tools that integrate with the Apache HTTP Server. In particular, the

---

3.   http://httpd.apache.org/ABOUT_APACHE.html

Apache JServ Protocol (AJP) connector can greatly improve how Apache communicates with our application.

The AJP connector creates a very fast connection between an Apache HTTP Server and Java servlet container (such as Tomcat). In addition to being fast, the connection is also secure. This is accomplished with two mechanisms:

Binary protocol

AJP is a packet-oriented protocol. This means that the web server communicates with its connector in binary format instead of a more readable plain-text format. This is also what makes it possible to secure the connection without incurring overhead.

Persistent TCP connections

The Apache HTTP server is able to keep a connection open across multiple requests/response cycles. This cuts down on the expensive process of socket creation. The AJP protocol supports a ping request that can be sent to connectors, allowing the web server to monitor its connections.

Let's configure Trinidad to listen with the AJP connector by adding the following entry to our config/trinidad.yml file:

Trinidad/twitalytics/config/trinidad.yml
```
ajp:
  port: 8099
```

Now when we start the server with the trinidad command, we'll see this in the console:

```
2011-11-30 06:45:17 INFO: Starting ProtocolHandler ["ajp-bio-8099"]
2011-11-30 06:45:17 INFO: Starting ProtocolHandler ["http-bio-3000"]
```

Tools like curl and our web browser don't support the AJP protocol, so we can't test the new connector with our regular methods. Instead, we'll need to connect Apache to our AJP port.

Apache can't connect with AJP out of the box. So, we'll have to install the mod_proxy_ajp extension. As with all of our other infrastructure, we'll configure this with Puppet. Open the puppet/modules/apache2/manifests/init.pp file, and add the following resource to it:

Trinidad/twitalytics/puppet/modules/apache2/manifests/init.pp
```
exec { "a2enmod proxy_ajp" :
  command => "a2enmod proxy_ajp",
  path => $path,
  require => Package["apache2"],
  unless => "apache2ctl -M | grep proxy_ajp"
}
```

Next, we'll need to modify the /etc/apache2/httpd.conf file on our virtual machine. This is where we will configure the proxy settings for Apache. We'll use a Puppet template to do this, so we'll need to create a templates directory.

```
$ mkdir puppet/modules/apache2/templates
```

Now let's create a puppet/modules/apache2/templates/httpd.conf.erb file and put the following content in it:

Trinidad/twitalytics/puppet/modules/apache2/templates/httpd.conf.erb
```
<VirtualHost *:80 >
    ProxyPass / ajp://<%= hostname %>:<%= port %>/
    ProxyPassReverse / ajp://<%= hostname %>:<%= port %>/
</VirtualHost>
```

We've configured our hostname and port with ERb tags so that the values can be passed into the template generator.

Now we'll add a resource to our manifest that turns the template into a real file on our virtual machine, but this time we'll wrap it in a function instead of making it freestanding. This will give us a little more flexibility in how we define the hostname and port values.

Open the puppet/modules/apache2/manifests/init.pp file, and add the following function to the apache2 class:

Trinidad/twitalytics/puppet/modules/apache2/manifests/init.pp
```
define apache2::httpd_conf($hostname="localhost", $port="8099") {
  file { $name :
    content => template("apache2/httpd.conf.erb")
  }
}
```

Now we can add a resource that invokes the previous function and declare a dependency on the "a2enmod proxy_ajp" resource.

Trinidad/twitalytics/puppet/modules/apache2/manifests/init.pp
```
apache2::httpd_conf { "/etc/apache2/httpd.conf":
  require => Exec["a2enmod proxy_ajp"]
}
```

That completes our httpd.conf setup, but we also need to make some changes to the security settings in the /etc/apache2/mods-enabled/proxy.conf file. We'll use a template for this, too. Create a proxy.conf.erb file in the templates directory, and add the following content to it:

Trinidad/twitalytics/puppet/modules/apache2/templates/proxy.conf.erb
```
<IfModule mod_proxy.c>
    ProxyRequests Off
    <Proxy *>
```

```
        AddDefaultCharset off
        Order deny,allow
        #Deny from all
        #Allow from .example.com
    </Proxy>
    ProxyVia On
</IfModule>
```

The majority of this template is boilerplate. The one significant change we're making is to comment out the following line:

Trinidad/twitalytics/puppet/modules/apache2/templates/proxy.conf.erb
```
#Deny from all
```

This enables unrestricted access to our proxy, which is fine in our local environment. In the real world, we would probably use ERb tags to inject some more detailed configuration like we did with the httpd.conf file. But that configuration would be specific to each environment, so we'll leave it wide open for now.

Next, we'll need a resource for this template. Add the following code to the puppet/modules/apache2/manifests/init.pp file:

Trinidad/twitalytics/puppet/modules/apache2/manifests/init.pp
```
file { "/etc/apache2/mods-enabled/proxy.conf":
  content => template("apache2/proxy.conf.erb"),
  require => File["/etc/apache2/httpd.conf"]
}
```

Finally, we need to add a new dependency to our Apache service resource. This will ensure that it's started after we've replaced the configuration files.

Trinidad/twitalytics/puppet/modules/apache2/manifests/init.pp
```
service { "apache2":
  ensure => running,
  require => [Package["apache2"], File["/etc/apache2/mods-enabled/proxy.conf"]]
}
```

Great, now we're ready to run the provisioning process again.

```
$ vagrant provision
...
[default] notice: /Stage[main]/Apache2/Exec[a2enmod proxy_ajp]/returns: executed ...
...
[default] notice: Finished catalog run in 168.07 seconds
```

Next, we'll deploy the Trinidad configuration changes and test things again.

```
$ cap deploy
...
```

Now point a browser to http://localhost:8000, and we'll see Twitalytics through the Apache AJP proxy.

In this simple example, the AJP connector doesn't provide a large amount of value over a traditional HTTP connector because we are running Apache and Trinidad on the same machine. The two servers are communicating with the loopback interface, which means there is little security risk and latency, so an encrypted binary protocol doesn't bring much to the party.

But if we needed to expand our deployment into a distributed cluster, the benefits of the AJP connector would start to be realized. This architecture for such a system is illustrated Figure 14, *A Trinidad cluster using the AJP connector*, on page 95. To implement this architecture, we would need to install the mod_proxy_balancer extension and modify our httpd.conf to look something like this:

```
<Proxy balancer://trinidad>
  BalancerMember ajp://server1:8099
  BalancerMember ajp://server2:8099
  BalancerMember ajp://server3:8099
</Proxy>

ProxyPass / balancer://trinidad/
```

We're really starting to take advantage of JRuby now, but we've put a lot of effort into setting up infrastructure components like Apache, Capistrano, Redis, and more. Before we move on to a new framework that simplifies our infrastructure, let's explore some alternative Trinidad deployment options that don't require us to be responsible for all of these tools.

5.5 Choosing Alternative Deployment Strategies

The deployment strategy we've used in this chapter packages the code in our environment and pushes it out to a production server. This pattern could be used from a CI server that checks out the code, runs the unit tests, integration tests, and finally deploys. But many shops prefer to deploy directly from a Git repository.

We could modify the Capistrano script we wrote earlier to deploy from a Git repository by changing the :scm and :repository attributes to something like this:

```
set :scm, :git
set :repository, "git://github.com/deployingjruby/twitalytics.git"
```

But some other deployment strategies become available to us when we start using Git. Let's take a look at two of them.

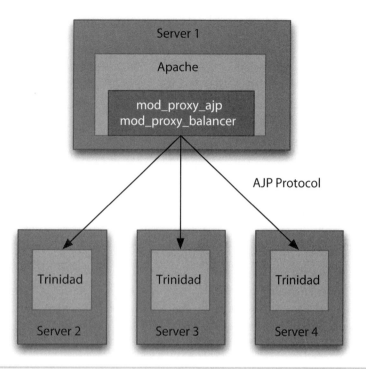

Figure 14—A Trinidad cluster using the AJP connector

Using the Management Console

As we discussed in Chapter 4, *Creating a Trinidad Application*, on page 57, the trinidad_sandbox_extension extension provides a management console, which gives us a little insight into our Trinidad configuration and a new mechanism for deploying applications. In particular, it allows us to deploy to a running Trinidad instance directly from a Git repository.

Let's install the trinidad_sandbox_extension by adding the gem to our application's configuration. Append the following statement to our Gemfile, and run bundle install.

Trinidad/twitalytics/Gemfile
```
gem 'trinidad_sandbox_extension'
```

Next, add the extension to the config/trinidad.yml file under the extensions: attribute.

Trinidad/twitalytics/config/trinidad.yml
```
sandbox:
  username: admin
  password: Passw0rd
  work_dir: 'work/sandbox'
```

The sandbox extension supports basic HTTP authentication, so we've set the username and password it will use.

Let's test it locally by starting the server with the trinidad command and browsing to http://localhost:3000/sandbox. Once we provide the username and password set earlier, we'll see the web page illustrated in Figure 15, *The Trinidad management console*, on page 97.

The management console gives us some basic information about the running state of each application deployed to Trinidad. It also gives us a REST API for querying, restarting, and stopping each application.

Now we need to deploy our changes to the production server with the cap deploy command. When it's completed, point your browser to http://localhost:8888/sandbox, and you'll see the same web page we saw on our development environment.

Next, follow the Deploy link, which will take us to the form shown in Figure 16, *Trinidad sandbox extension*, on page 98. Fill in the fields with the URL git://github.com/deployingjruby/twitalytics.git, the master branch, and assign it to the twitalytics context path. Click the Deploy button, and the application will be pulled from the Git repo.

We could choose to statically configure Trinidad, rather than provide a trinidad.yml file with our application. If we did, the trinidad_sandbox_extension would allow us to eliminate our Capistrano scripts. But we would still need to configure our deployment environment with numerous components and make sure all required gems had been installed. If we really want to simplify things, then we need to deploy our application to the cloud.

Deploying to the Cloud

There are very few cloud-based services that support JRuby applications. In Chapter 3, *Deploying an Archive File*, on page 37, you learned about one of the Java-based cloud services that supports JRuby WAR files. In this section, we'll deploy Twitalytics to Engine Yard,[4] which provides excellent support for both JRuby and Trinidad.

Engine Yard has been a major JRuby proponent for a number of years. When Oracle acquired Sun in 2010, Engine Yard took advantage of the project's uncertainty by offering jobs to the JRuby core team. Since then, JRuby and many of its related libraries have been able to flourish because of the commercial support.

---

4. http://www.engineyard.com/

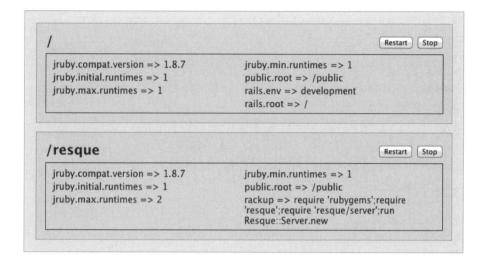

Figure 15—The Trinidad management console

Let's test Engine Yard's platform by deploying Twitalytics to it. But before doing so, we'll need to create a Git repository that Engine Yard can access. You may choose from a number of platforms to host it, including GitHub[5] and Bitbucket.[6] Once the remote repository has been created, we'll have to make a few changes to our application to get it ready for Engine Yard.

Engine Yard's Cloud Managed Trinidad service is relatively new, but it supports most Trinidad features. One feature that it does not support is running multiple applications in the same container. That means we won't be able to run our Resque console or the Sandbox console in the same runtime as Twitalytics. We'll need to remove the sandbox: attribute from the trinidad.yml file, and we can disable the Resque console by adding the disable_web: attribute to the Resque extensions configuration in the same file. We also need to remove the AJP configuration. Engine Yard uses Nginx and the Tomcat HTTP connector, so the AJP connector will interfere with our stack. After these changes, our complete trinidad.yml file should look like this:

---

5. https://github.com/
6. https://bitbucket.org/

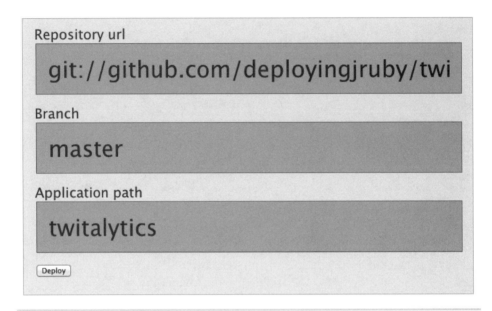

Figure 16—Trinidad sandbox extension

```
Trinidad/ey/config/trinidad.yml
jruby_max_runtimes: 1
extensions:
  diagnostics:
  scheduler:
  resque:
    path: 'lib/workers'
    queues: critical, normal, low
    count:  1
    redis_host: 'localhost:6379'
    work_dir: 'work/resque'
    disable_web: true
```

Now we're ready to set up our Engine Yard instance. Browse to the Engine Yard website and create a new account and a new application. When creating the application, be sure to select JRuby as the runtime and Trinidad as the platform.

Now we'll use the Engine Yard gem to deploy our code, but we need to install it first.

Traditional Deployment with Heroku

Heroku is a cloud deployment platform that provides support for Java web applications as part of its Cedar stack,[a] which means it's possible to run any Rack-based JRuby application.[b]

Heroku does not use Trinidad, Warbler, or any of the frameworks we'll discuss in this book. Instead, you'll have to add a little bit of XML to your application's configuration in the form of a Maven pom.xml file. But other than that, a basic Rails or Rack application can remain pretty much the same.

Instead of using Capistrano, Heroku pulls code from a Git repository. Once an application has been created, you can deploy to it by pushing to the Heroku repository with a command like this:

```
$ git push heroku master
```

The Heroku server will use a post-receive hook to deploy the application after your push. Other than the additional XML configuration, this is basically the same as deploying an MRI-based application.

Because Heroku is a heavily managed platform, the benefits of the JVM are somewhat hidden. A Heroku application is scaled up by adding new *dynos*, which are something like operating system processes. The main advantage is that you can use Java libraries and threading.

---

a.   http://devcenter.heroku.com/articles/java
b.   http://blog.heroku.com/archives/2011/8/25/java/

```
$ gem install engineyard
Fetching: engineyard-serverside-adapter-1.5.21.gem (100%)
Fetching: engineyard-1.4.15.gem (100%)

Welcome to Engine Yard!

Deploying for the first time? The Engine Yard Pandas want to help you!

Email pandas@engineyard.com with your questions or queries.
(Panda = 1. Polite Agent of Non-Destructive Assimilation; 2. Cute fluffy animal.)

We wish you every success with your business!

  - The Pandas

Successfully installed engineyard-serverside-adapter-1.5.21
Successfully installed engineyard-1.4.15
2 gems installed
```

This will add the ey command to our path. To use it, change directories to the checked-out copy of the application from the Git repository. Then run the deploy command.

```
$ ey deploy
Loading application data from EY Cloud...
Beginning deploy of ref 'ey' for 'twitalytics' in 'twitalytics_dev' on server...
Triggering deploy on deploy@ec2-0-0-0-0.compute-1.amazonaws.com.
Successfully installed engineyard-serverside-1.5.21
1 gem installed
Triggering deploy on deploy@ec2-0-0-0-0.compute-1.amazonaws.com.
...
Successful deployment recorded in EY Cloud
Deploy complete
Now you can run `ey launch' to open the application in a browser.
```

The first time we run this command, it will ask for our username and password so it can fetch our API token. But it will save this, and subsequent runs won't need the credentials. When the command completes, we can view the application by running this command:

```
$ ey launch
```

Great. Twitalytics has been deployed on the Engine Yard stack, and all of the system configuration was handled for us. If cloud deployment is an option for your organization, it can save a great number of maintenance headaches.

5.6 Wrapping Up

We've created an environment that is similar to traditional Ruby deployment environments, but it has come at a cost. Our setup is complex, and we still have multiple processes because of our Redis server.

We're using Capistrano, which is helpful because it's familiar. But Capistrano is a tool that works around the problems created by traditional deployment. We're not actually solving them. We have no standard packaging format for deploying our application, so we have to use outside tools to push our changes (such as Git and tar). We also have a lot of infrastructure to control, which complicates our recipe.

In Chapter 1, *Getting Started with JRuby*, on page 1, we saw how Warbler fixed the packaging problem by using a WAR file, but it left our background tasks and scheduled jobs out of the application. They had to be supported by external processes and tools. Trinidad incorporated those external parts into our application, but we are still cobbling our application together from disparate parts.

We want a more cohesive application that's easy to deploy. It would make our infrastructure less complex and more manageable. In the next chapter, you'll learn about a platform that provides not only a web server but an entire application server. It will eliminate our need for external tools like Redis, which make it difficult to monitor the health of our system.

Let's finish our JRuby deployment by running Twitalytics on an application server.

CHAPTER 6

Creating a TorqueBox Application

Traditional deployment with Trinidad has been a great solution for Twitalytics thus far. It simplified our infrastructure and deployment. But as our website continues to grow in popularity, our need to scale has grown too. Running Twitalytics on a single server is not sufficient anymore; we need a cluster.

We can already run Twitalytics on multiple servers with Trinidad and Warbler by using Apache to load balance them. But this is not a true cluster because each of the nodes is unaware of the other nodes. This is a problem when we have lots of asynchronous jobs like Twitalytics does. We need these background jobs to coordinate with each other. Fortunately for us, TorqueBox can do this.

TorqueBox is the most powerful deployment environment available to any Ruby application. It's capable of boosting performance without even changing a single line of code.[1] But it also has features that can improve the way an application is composed.

TorqueBox provides built-in support for clustering, which allows distributed servers to replicate session data, coordinate jobs, and send messages to each other. This will help Twitalytics scale up without incurring the overhead of additional infrastructure. In this chapter, we'll port Twitalytics onto TorqueBox and start taking advantage of this power. But we'll also leverage TorqueBox's support for bidirectional communication between a client and server to add some new features to the application. Then we'll use TorqueBox's centralized management console to monitor each of these moving parts. In the coming chapters, we'll put this all together and deploy Twitalytics to a working cluster.

Because of its built-in support for features such as clustering, TorqueBox is often distinguished as enterprise-grade software. But it does this without any

---

1. http://torquebox.org/news/2011/10/06/torquebox-2x-performance/

of the drawbacks we programmers often associate with "enterprisey" things. These built-in features include the following:

- Long-running services (daemons)
- Scheduled jobs (like cron)
- Background jobs
- Session replication across a cluster
- Distributed caching across a cluster
- Distributed transactions

The Twitalytics application is not enterprise software, but it has a need for all of the features we listed earlier. In fact, any application that is successful will eventually need these capabilities. Having them integrated into our platform results in a more cohesive, reliable, and manageable environment. This kind of platform is called an *application server*.

6.1 What Is an Application Server?

An application server is a different kind of platform from what most Rubyists are familiar with. Traditionally, a Ruby application is responsible for gathering together the libraries and tools it needs to run. For example, if our application needs to listen on port 3000, then it pulls in a library to handle HTTP listening. This kind of architecture is illustrated in Figure 17, *Traditional Ruby application architecture*, on page 105. But why should our application care that it listens on port 3000? Shouldn't our application be focused on solving the problem it was created for?

In Chapter 3, *Deploying an Archive File*, on page 37, we solved this problem by using Apache Tomcat to invert the way we deployed. Instead of running our application, we ran the Tomcat container and deployed an archive file into it. This decoupled our application from the job of listening on an HTTP port. But there many other problems in our architecture like this one, and they can't be solved by Tomcat alone.

Ruby applications deal with many concerns like HTTP listening that are outside the scope of their business requirements. Messaging is another example. When Twitalytics needed to run a process asynchronously in the background, we pulled in Resque and integrated with it. Even worse, our application needed to manage and monitor the Resque processes!

The cumbersome chore of assembling our infrastructure this way doesn't conform to traditional Ruby principles. Ruby is designed to be productive and fun. That's why libraries like Rails are designed to get low-level details out of

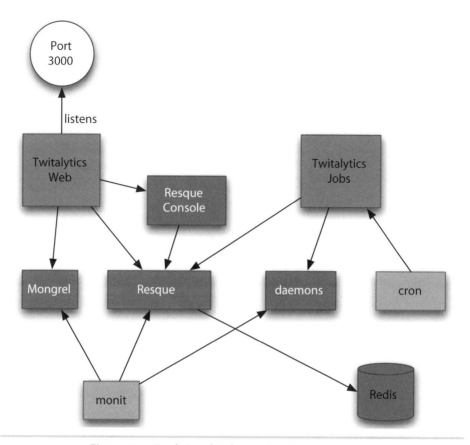

Figure 17—Traditional Ruby application architecture

the way—so we can focus on writing business logic. But why do we still have to set up, integrate, and monitor a framework that runs background processes? We need a container with an attitude.

A container could handle these things for us by isolating the infrastructure components from our application and moving them into a cohesive platform layer beneath our business logic. Tomcat began to do this for us, but it handled only web requests. We need something more comprehensive that can provide the infrastructure for an entire application. This kind of container, which is illustrated in Figure 18, *Ruby application server architecture*, on page 106, is called an *application server*.

TorqueBox is a Ruby application server, and it's the only one of its kind. Let's port Twitalytics onto this platform as the last step in rescuing it.

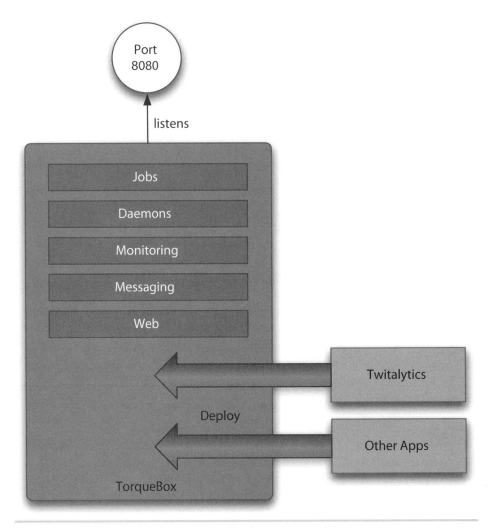

Figure 18—Ruby application server architecture

6.2 Getting Started with TorqueBox

TorqueBox is distributed as both a gem and a binary file. We'll use the gem on our development machines, so we'll need to install it with the following command:

```
$ gem install torquebox-server
...
```

This will add the torquebox executable to our path. We can run it without any arguments to get a list of available tasks.

```
$ torquebox
Tasks:
  torquebox deploy ROOT     # Deploy an application to TorqueBox
  torquebox undeploy ROOT   # Undeploy an application from TorqueBox
  torquebox run             # Run TorqueBox (binds to localhost, use -b to ov...
  torquebox rails ROOT      # Create a Rails application at ROOT using the To...
  torquebox archive ROOT    # Create a nice self-contained application archive
  torquebox cli             # Run the JBoss AS7 CLI
  torquebox env [VARIABLE]  # Display TorqueBox environment variables
  torquebox help [TASK]     # Describe available tasks or one specific task
  torquebox list            # List applications deployed to TorqueBox and the..
```

Let's use the env task to display the location where TorqueBox is installed.

```
$ torquebox env TORQUEBOX_HOME
~/.rvm/gems/jruby-1.6.7/gems/torquebox-server-2.0.2-java
```

Before we use any other tasks, let's create and check out a torquebox branch that's based on the jruby branch we created in Chapter 1, *Getting Started with JRuby*, on page 1.

```
$ cd ~/code/twitalytics
$ git checkout -b torquebox jruby
```

We don't need to make any changes to the code to run the basic web application, so let's start the TorqueBox server with the run task.

```
$ torquebox run
...
```

This will generate a lot of console output. When TorqueBox boots, it initializes all the components that support the features we described at the beginning of the chapter. But amazingly, it does this in a relatively short time.

TorqueBox is running, but our application has not been deployed. Because TorqueBox is an application server, it can run independently of any application. This differs from traditional Ruby web servers, which are booted to run a single application and start it up immediately. We'll leave the TorqueBox server running as we deploy Twitalytics and other applications to it, so we'll need to open a new terminal and move to the Twitalytics directory. We can deploy Twitalytics to TorqueBox with the following command:

```
$ torquebox deploy
Deployed: twitalytics-knob.yml
    into: ~/.rvm/gems/jruby-1.6.7/gems/torquebox-server-2.0.2-java/...
```

Now we'll see the application running when we browse to http://localhost:8080, and we'll also see some information in the TorqueBox console (the first terminal session) that lets us know the deployment was successful.

Let's take a closer look at the output of the deploy task. It tells us that TorqueBox created a twitalytics-knob.yml file and deployed it into the jboss/stan-dalone/deployments directory under TORQUEBOX_HOME. This YAML file is the deployment descriptor for our application, which tells TorqueBox where our application is located on the file system. In Section 6.3, *Creating a Deployment Descriptor*, on page 109, we'll create a custom descriptor and add some advanced configuration to it, but the default descriptor will work for now.

We have a Rails application running on TorqueBox, and it's nice that we didn't need to modify the code from our JRuby branch to do this. But we'll need to add some configuration if we want to take advantage of the more advanced TorqueBox features such as background jobs and distributed session caching. Fortunately, TorqueBox provides a Rails template that can create this config-uration in one command.

```
$ rake rails:template \
LOCATION=`torquebox env TORQUEBOX_HOME`/share/rails/template.rb
      gemfile   torquebox-rake-support
      gemfile   torquebox
       remove   config/initializers/session_store.rb
  initializer   session_store.rb
  initializer   active_record_backgroundable.rb
     rakefile   torquebox.rake
```

This added two dependencies to our Gemfile. The first provides a set of Rake tasks that can be used to deploy the application in lieu of the torquebox com-mand. The configuration of those tasks is contained in the torquebox.rake file. The second new dependency is the torquebox gem, which is actually very lightweight but has dependencies on several other gems that provide TorqueBox's messaging and clustering features.

The template also removed our existing session_store.rb initializer and replaced it with a file that enables the server-based, in-memory, cluster-compatible TorqueBox session store.

Finally, the template added an active_record_backgroundable.rb initializer, which adds some new capabilities to ActiveRecord::Base. We'll use this later, too.

Let's run Bundler so it can install our new dependencies.

```
$ bundle install
...
Using torquebox-core (2.0.2)
Using torquebox-transactions (2.0.2)
Using torquebox-cache (2.0.2)
Using torquebox-configure (2.0.2)
Using torquebox-messaging (2.0.2)
```

```
Using torquebox-naming (2.0.2)
Using torquebox-rake-support (2.0.2)
Using torquebox-security (2.0.2)
Using torquebox-stomp (2.0.2)
Using torquebox-web (2.0.2)
Using torquebox (2.0.2)
...
```

Now let's enhance our configuration with a custom descriptor that will allow us to tailor how the components in our system work together.

6.3 Creating a Deployment Descriptor

A TorqueBox deployment descriptor is a configuration file that defines how the components of the application server get wired together at deployment time. Earlier in the chapter, we saw how TorqueBox used a YAML-based deployment descriptor to notify the server of our application. This external descriptor contained the default configuration for a TorqueBox application. But we can override these defaults by creating a descriptor that is internal to our application.

An internal deployment descriptor can be in either YAML or Ruby format. We'll use the Ruby format because it provides a more expressive DSL. In the config directory of our application, we'll create a torquebox.rb file and add the following code to it:

```
TorqueBox.configure do
  # TODO add some configuration
end
```

TorqueBox will look for this file when it boots our application and use the configure block to override its default settings. We can specify a number of directives within this block that will be applied to the various TorqueBox subsystems. These subsystems include the following:

Web
    Configures the part of the application that handles web requests

Jobs
    Allows us to schedule recurring jobs

Messaging
    Configures how background messages are distributed and processed

Services
    Defines long-running background jobs

In addition to the subsystems, we can also configure environment variables, Ruby runtime options, and how application runtimes are pooled. We'll start by configuring a runtime pool.

TorqueBox pools application instances just like the ones we described for Warbler and Trinidad. Because Twitalytics is thread-safe, we want to use a shared pool. A shared pool is a false pool, which means that it contains a single instance of our application that is shared between threads. We can do this by adding a call to the pool directive.

TorqueBox/twitalytics/config/torquebox.rb
```
TorqueBox.configure do
  pool :web, :type => :shared
end
```

A shared pool is the TorqueBox default for any environment other than development, so this configuration won't actually change much. It's also important to point out that this pool applies only to the web subsystem. As we add more subsystems to our application, we can define their pools independently. This provides a good way to isolate potentially non-thread-safe code.

Because our application is running on Rails, we have to do more than configure TorqueBox to use a shared pool. We also need to configure Rails to run in thread-safe mode, as we did for Warbler and Trinidad. We do this by uncommenting the following line in our config/environments/production.rb file:

TorqueBox/twitalytics/config/environments/production.rb
```
config.threadsafe!
```

TorqueBox is aware of this Rails configuration, so setting both the pool value and config.threadsafe! is actually redundant.

Now we can deploy Twitalytics again with the torquebox deploy command. When the application boots, it will be using a shared pool (single instance) for the web runtime. But how do we know that is what it's actually doing? At the least, it would be nice to inspect the pool to ensure it's configured correctly without depending on the log file. This is important when using a shared pool, but it's especially important when using a pool containing multiple application instances. If TorqueBox hits our pool's ceiling too quickly, it may be a sign that we need to increase our maximum value. It's difficult to identify the pool's growth rate from a log file, so let's install a tool that will provide some visibility into our server.

6.4 Using the Management Console

The TorqueBox project includes a management console called BackStage that we can deploy alongside our applications to provide visibility into all components of the server.

BackStage is distributed as a gem, so we can use the following command to install it:

```
$ gem install torquebox-backstage
...
```

This adds a backstage executable to our path that we can use to deploy the console application like this:

```
$ TORQUEBOX_HOME=`torquebox env torquebox_home` backstage deploy
>> WARNING: deploying BackStage with no security - use the --secure=username ...
>> Deployed torquebox-backstage-knob.yml to ~/.rvm/gems/jruby-1.6.7/gems/tor ...
```

The warning message tells us that BackStage is running without any security. That's OK for our development machine, but we'll lock it down when we deploy to production. The second line tells us that the BackStage application deployed successfully. When we browse to http://localhost:8080/backstage, we'll see Figure 19, *The BackStage dashboard*, on page 112.

Next, we can follow the Runtime Pools link to get some more detailed information on our web runtime. The page will display a list of runtime pools, as pictured in Figure 20, *The BackStage Runtime Pools page*, on page 112.

There are two web pools: one for Twitalytics and one for BackStage. Both of them are running in the same container but are completely isolated. Even if the two applications have conflicting gem dependencies, they can still run alongside each other. We can even deploy an application that uses Ruby 1.8 alongside an application that uses Ruby 1.9. This is all possible because of the separate runtimes.

In addition to inspecting the runtime pools, we can use BackStage to check each of the subsystems. Let's move on and start making use of these.

6.5 Scheduling a Recurring Job

Jobs are components that execute on a schedule instead of in response to user action. In the case of Twitalytics, the schedule is recurring, but other jobs could be a one-time event. With TorqueBox, jobs like this run asynchronously in the background, but they still execute within the same JVM process as the rest of the application.

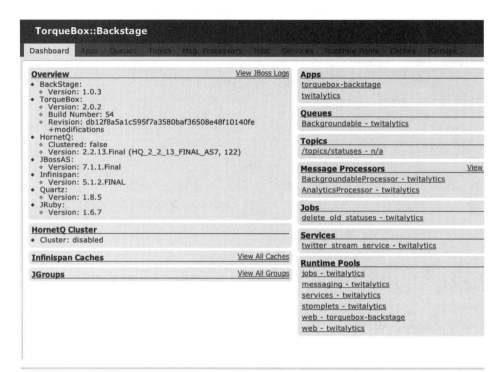

Figure 19—The BackStage dashboard

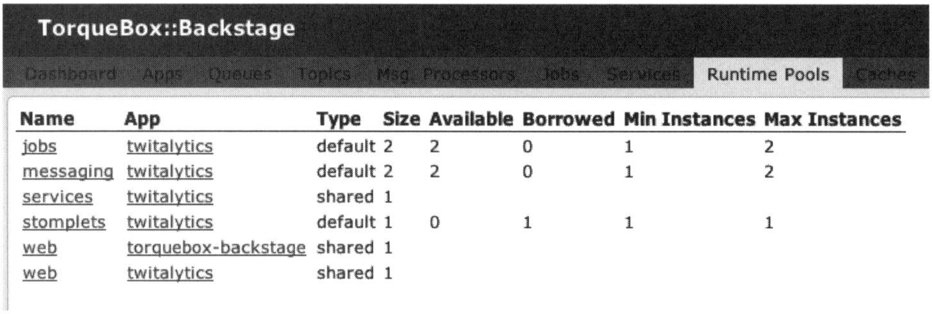

Figure 20—The BackStage Runtime Pools page

The Twitalytics recurring job removes old status updates from the database. In Chapter 4, *Creating a Trinidad Application*, on page 57, we ported this job to Trinidad. Now, we'll port it to TorqueBox.

The job is located in the lib/jobs/delete_old_statuses.rb file, and it looks like this:

twitalytics/lib/jobs/delete_old_statuses.rb
```
class DeleteOldStatuses
```

```
  def run
    ids = Status.where("created_at < ?", 30.days.ago)
    if ids.size > 0
      Status.destroy(ids)
      puts "#{ids.size} statuses have been deleted!"
    else
      puts "No statuses have been deleted."
    end
  end
end
DeleteOldStatuses.new.run
```

When Twitalytics was running on MRI, this background job was scheduled by adding a crontab entry and having the cron daemon run the script with the rails runner command. But that increased the complexity of our infrastructure (since cron became another dependency) and made it less portable because there is no cron on Windows. We improved this with Trinidad by using the Scheduler extension, which uses the same Quartz[2] library as TorqueBox's scheduler. But neither Trinidad's scheduled jobs nor cron can scale like TorqueBox schedule jobs. We'll see this in more detail in Chapter 8, *Clustering a TorqueBox Application*, on page 149, but we'll begin by getting our jobs running on TorqueBox.

First, we'll move this job to a new location under the app/jobs directory. We'll use the git mv command so the repository stays in sync with our changes.

```
$ git mv lib/jobs/delete_old_statuses.rb app/jobs/
```

TorqueBox will pick up any jobs located in the app/jobs directory and run them with the full context of the application. That means it will have access to our ActiveRecord models without relying on rails runner or anything like that.

Next, we need to remove the following statement that instantiates the Delete-OldStatuses class.

twitalytics/lib/jobs/delete_old_statuses.rb
```
DeleteOldStatuses.new.run
```

TorqueBox will do this for us as long as we have a no-argument constructor. It also expects our job class to have a no-argument run() method, which will perform the job's work when invoked. Our class already has both of these, so we are all set.

---

2.   http://quartz-scheduler.org/

Next, we need to schedule the job by adding an entry to the config/torquebox.rb file. We'll use the job() directive and pass it the class name and a crontab-like value.

```
job DeleteOldStatuses do
  cron "0 0/5 * * * ?"
end
```

Let's deploy the application to the TorqueBox server again. If it isn't already running, we'll need to start it in a separate terminal with the torquebox run task. Then we can deploy with the torquebox deploy task.

After the application has booted, we'll see some output in the console like this:

```
21:17:05,112 INFO  [stdout] ... No statuses have been deleted.
21:17:10,080 INFO  [stdout] ... No statuses have been deleted.
```

Our job is running on a schedule. Now let's enhance its configuration.

The DeleteOldStatuses class has the age threshold hard-coded to 30.days.ago, but it would be better if this value were defined as part of our job configuration. We can do this by adding a config() directive to our job() block.

```
job DeleteOldStatuses do
  cron "0 0/5 * * * ?"
  config do
    max_age 30
  end
end
```

Next, we need to add an initialize(options={}) method to our class that accepts a Hash of options as an argument.

```
def initialize(options = {})
  @max_age = options["max_age"]
  @max_age ||= 30
end
```

Now we can use the @max_age variable in our run() method.

```
ids = Status.where("created_at < ?", @max_age.days.ago)
```

When we deploy the application again, it will use the configuration option.

Having the recurring job deployed as part of our TorqueBox configuration means not only that it runs as part of our application process but that we can use the same TorqueBox clustering, monitoring, and management tools for it as we will for the rest of the application.

Let's take a look at the job in our management console. Browse to the Back-Stage dashboard at http://localhost:8080/backstage, and then click the Jobs link. We'll see an entry for the DeleteOldStatuses job like in Figure 21, *The BackStage Jobs page*, on page 116.

We can see that our job is being scheduled, and we can even use the Stop button to unschedule it. Go ahead and try it. The Stop button will be replaced by a Start button that you can use to bring the job back up.

Our job is all set to delete old Status records. Now let's use some of the other TorqueBox subsystems to create Status records.

6.6   Creating a Long-Running Daemon

TorqueBox provides a built-in framework for executing long-running daemons, which it calls *services*. Like scheduled jobs, services run within the same process as the rest of the application, and they get access to the full application environment.

Twitalytics doesn't have any long-running jobs, but that's primarily because they would have complicated our infrastructure. In most MRI application environments, it's common to leverage the operating system's support for daemons or use some third-party library. This results in a need for more tools, such as god and monit, to monitor these processes. Now that we are using TorqueBox, adding a service to Twitalytics won't require any new tools or libraries.

Because Twitalytics didn't have any long-running jobs, it used a lazy strategy for creating statuses. Each time the Customers page was loaded, a request was made to Twitter to get the latest tweets. This can be seen in the index() action of the CustomersController.

Lazily loading tweets meant that the application missed a lot of tweets if no one loaded the page. It also made the page take longer to load because it had to hit the remote service synchronously with the HTTP request.

We can fix these problems by eagerly fetching tweets from Twitter in the background with a service. This will effectively create a stream of near-real-time tweets into the Twitalytics database.

Let's begin by creating a directory for the service.

```
$ mkdir app/services
```

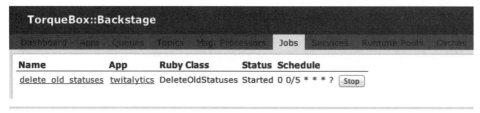

Figure 21—The BackStage Jobs page

Next, we'll create a twitter_stream_service.rb file in the new directory and add the basic framework for our service class to it.

TorqueBox/twitalytics/app/services/twitter_stream_service.rb
```
class TwitterStreamService

  def initialize(opts={})
  end

  def start
    @thread = Thread.new do
    end
  end

  def stop
  end

end
```

All of these methods need to return quickly, which is why the start method will typically spawn another thread or start an event loop to accomplish the long-running tasks.

Next, we need to add an instance variable to the initialize() method that will be used as a flag to stop our service.

TorqueBox/twitalytics/app/services/twitter_stream_service.rb
```
def initialize(opts={})
  @done = false
end
```

Now we can get into the meat of the service. We're going to use the TwitterUtil module in our lib directory, so we'll need to include this in our service class.

TorqueBox/twitalytics/app/services/twitter_stream_service.rb
```
class TwitterStreamService
  include TwitterUtil
```

We also need to add the code that uses the Twitter API to the start() method.

TorqueBox/twitalytics/app/services/twitter_stream_service.rb

```
def start
  @thread = Thread.new do
    begin
      Status.find_or_create_from(
        fetch_tweets_since(since_id ||= nil) do |status|
          since_id = status["id"]
        end
      )
    end until @done
  end
end
```

The fetch_tweets_since(since_id) method will collect all the new tweets since the one provided as an argument. We're returning all of those to the Status.find_or_create_from(statuses) method, which will create new database records.

Next, we need to add the proper calls to clean up when our service terminates. We can do this by adding the following statements to the stop() method:

TorqueBox/twitalytics/app/services/twitter_stream_service.rb

```
def stop
  @done = true
  @thread.join
end
```

Now we're ready to add the service to our configuration. Open the config/torquebox.rb file, and add the following service() directive to the configure() block:

TorqueBox/twitalytics/config/torquebox.rb

```
service TwitterStreamService
```

Let's deploy our configuration changes with the torquebox deploy task. If the TorqueBox server is not already running, then we'll also need to start with the torquebox run task. We can look at BackStage to see whether it's running. In Figure 22, *The BackStage Services page*, on page 118, we can see how BackStage will list our long-running daemon and its status.

Our service is running, and it's streaming real tweets from Twitter. Because the service creates statuses in the database, there isn't any need for our CustomersController to fetch statuses each time we load the page. We'll replace this call in the index() action with a query to get the latest twenty records.

TorqueBox/twitalytics/app/controllers/customers_controller.rb

```
def index
  @statuses = Status.find(:all, :order => "created_at desc", :limit => 20)
end
```

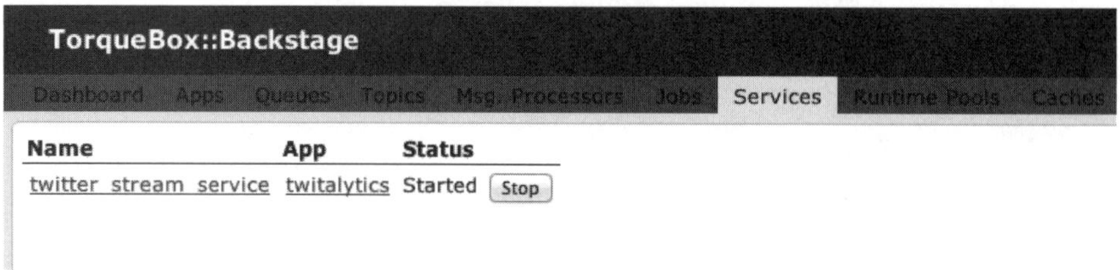

Figure 22—The BackStage Services page

Fetching the records from our local database will be much faster than pulling from Twitter, so the Customer page will load quicker than it did before. Point a browser to http://localhost:8080/customers/index, and you'll see the most recent tweets.

As you'll recall from Chapter 4, *Creating a Trinidad Application*, on page 57, each time we create new Status objects, a background job is supposed to run some analytics against them. Our existing implementation of this background job uses Resque, but now that we are running on TorqueBox, we can use the built-in messaging subsystem to execute this job.

6.7 Running Background Jobs

TorqueBox provides several tools for running background jobs, all of which leverage TorqueBox's messaging subsystem. This subsystem is backed by the JBoss HornetQ[3] message broker, which is a robust, open source technology that comes ready for clustering, load balancing, failover, and other advanced features.

TorqueBox hides the underlying details of messaging system from us with varying levels of abstraction. This allows us to run jobs asynchronously without ever dealing with the components of a messaging system. But the more advanced constructs it provides give us the power of enterprise-class messaging.

Before we port our Resque tasks to TorqueBox, let's take a look at a simpler example of asynchronous processing.

Using Backgroundable Methods

The quickest way to create a background job in TorqueBox is with the Backgroundable class, which provides an interface that's similar to the get_back gem

---

3. http://www.jboss.org/hornetq

we used in Chapter 1, *Getting Started with JRuby*, on page 1. But its mechanism for executing background jobs is markedly different.

The get_back gem created a pool of threads that our background job borrowed from to do its work. As a result, there wasn't a good way to monitor the job or ensure its durability (that is, provide a guarantee that it would actually run in the event of a system crash during the job). TorqueBox's Backgroundable class ensures durability and allows us to configure how the job will be run and monitored.

To do this, we'll modify the Twitalytics feature for retweeting a public tweet so that it executes in the background. *Retweeting* is a Twitter term for reposting another user's status on our account so that our followers will see it. A Twitalytics user can retweet a customer's status by clicking one of the Retweet links on the Customers page. The existing implementation invokes the Twitter service synchronously, which blocks the user's browser. Because Twitter is an external and remote interface, this can often take long enough that the user closes the browser. We don't want users closing the browser that contains our website, so running the retweet function in the background is important.

We'll start by opening the file app/controllers/customers_controller.rb and looking at the retweet() action.

TorqueBox/twitalytics/app/controllers/customers_controller.rb
```
def retweet
  Status.find(params[:id]).retweet
  redirect_to customers_path
end
```

It fetches the Status resource corresponding to the status the user clicked and invokes the retweet() method on it. Let's take a look at that method, which can be found in the app/models/status.rb file.

TorqueBox/twitalytics/app/models/status.rb
```
def retweet
  sleep(10)
  # Twitter.update("RT @#{creator}: {status_text}")
  puts "Retweeting Status{id=#{id}}"
end
```

The application is only simulating the slow interaction with Twitter by sleeping the thread for ten seconds. To perform a real retweet, it would need an OAuth token, so this will have to suffice. We can demonstrate what happens by running the TorqueBox server, browsing to the http://localhost:8080/customers/index

page, and following one of the Retweet links. The browser hangs for ten seconds. After it returns, we'll see something like this in the TorqueBox console:

```
16:53:04,134 INFO  [stdout] ... Retweeting Status{id=1234}
```

To fix this, we'll use the always_background() method, which is available in all ActiveRecord::Base subclasses by virtue of the config/initializers/active_record_backgroundable.rb file. This initializer was added to our project by the TorqueBox Rails template, and because of it, we can add the following statement to the Status class immediately after the retweet() method (adding it after the method is not required; it can be added anywhere within the class definition):

TorqueBox/twitalytics/app/models/status.rb
```
always_background :retweet
```

Now, when the retweet() method is invoked, it will immediately return control to the caller and run the method asynchronously in the background.

The always_background() method does not accept a pool size argument like the get_back() method. Instead, we can configure this globally in our config/torquebox.rb file by adding the following statement to the configure() block:

TorqueBox/twitalytics/config/torquebox.rb
```
options_for Backgroundable, :concurrency => 10
```

The :concurrency option defines the maximum number of Backgroundable jobs that can run in parallel, effectively throttling the volume of retweets.

We can test this by running the server and following a Retweet link again. The browser will return immediately, and ten seconds later a statement will appear in the console. We'll also see some console output on the first invocation as the messaging subsystem initializes itself.

The always_background() method is convenient for cases where we want a particular method to always run asynchronously. But it's also possible to allow the caller to determine whether a method will run in the background. For example, we could have modified the retweet() action in the CustomersController as follows:

```
def retweet
  Status.find(params[:id]).background.retweet
  redirect_to customers_path
end
```

In this case, we have inserted a call to the background() method prior to invoking retweet(). This has the same effect as the always_background() method but on a per-invocation basis.

The Backgroundable methods for running background jobs are convenient but not terribly flexible. Furthermore, all background methods share the same runtime pool, so it's difficult to separate them from one another. For example, if we wanted to limit the concurrency of a method so that only one job ran at a time, it would limit the concurrency of all background methods using Backgroundable. As a result, Backgroundable won't be sufficient for running our analytics engine. Instead, we'll use a lower-level messaging abstraction called a *message processor*.

Creating a Message Processor

Message processors are Ruby classes that run in a separate thread of execution from the main runtime. Their job is to encapsulate any logic that needs to be run against messages that match a given pattern.

Message processors can be considered lower level than Backgroundable because they require that we explicitly define how they receive messages and how messages are sent to them. As a result, we'll need to understand the components of the messaging system in order to explain how message processors work.

The TorqueBox messaging subsystem is composed of the following components, as illustrated in Figure 23, *Components of the TorqueBox messaging system*, on page 122.

Messages
> A message is the unit of communication in the messaging system. It can be anything from a BLOB of octets to a serialized instance of an application model.

Producers and consumers
> Producers and consumers are the actors in a messaging system. They send and receive messages, respectively. In general, producers and consumers are unaware of each other, so they communicate through destinations. Message processors are primarily consumers, but they can also be producers.

Destinations
> Destinations are mailboxes for messages. Producers put messages in a mailbox, and consumers take them out. There are two kinds of destinations: queues and topics. Messages in a queue will be received by only one consumer, and messages in a topic will be received by all consumers listening to that mailbox. This is illustrated in Figure 24, *Queues vs. topics*, on page 123.

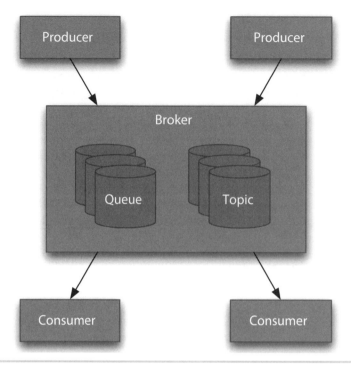

Figure 23—Components of the TorqueBox messaging system

Broker

The broker is the component in a messaging system that knows how to route messaging from a destination to one or more consumers. The TorqueBox message broker is provided by the JBoss HornetQ framework.

To use the messaging system for our analytics engine, we'll need to identify each of these components. We'll begin by defining our messages.

Because the analytics engine will be triggered by the creation of new statuses, we'll use the status objects as the body of each message. That's all we need to know about our message format for now.

Next, we'll create a destination for our messages. Open the config/torquebox.rb file, and add this statement to the configure() block:

```
topic "/topics/statuses"
```

We're using a topic because all of the consumers listening to this kind of destination will receive each message that is published to it. This is important because eventually we want to have more than just the analytics engine consume from this topic.

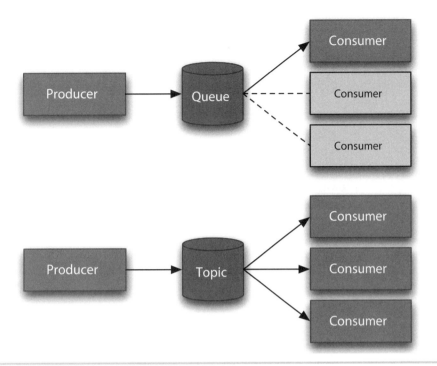

Figure 24—Queues vs. topics

Now we can use our destination by creating a producer. Because we want to publish this message each time new status objects are created, we'll use the Status class as a producer. This makes sense because it's also where we produced messages for our Resque workers. We'll start by providing the class with a handle to our destination. Open the app/models/status.rb file, and modify the beginning of the class so it looks like this:

TorqueBox/twitalytics/app/models/status.rb
```
class Status < ActiveRecord::Base
  extend TorqueBox::Injectors

  def self.topic
    @@topic ||= inject('/topics/statuses')
  end
```

The TorqueBox::Injectors module allows us to connect various components of our application together using a pattern called *injection*. This is common software architectural strategy because it moves the responsibility of finding and connecting components into the container, but it's not used very often in Ruby because the language is so dynamic that meta-programming techniques are favored instead. Injection provides many benefits over meta-programming, however. It allows the container to manage how and when the components become connected, which avoids problems like cyclic dependencies and components starting up in the wrong order.

Now that the Status class has a handle to the topic, we can replace the commented-out call to Resque.enqueue(UpdateAnalytics, r.map(&:id)) with the following code:

TorqueBox/twitalytics/app/models/status.rb
```
topic.publish r.to_json
```

This statement publishes a JSON message to our destination. We're using JSON because we'll need that format later, but TorqueBox does not require it. We could just pass the object as is, and TorqueBox would serialize it for us. We can even configure the encoding it uses.[4]

We've now defined the destination, messages, and producer for our job. We've discussed the HornetQ broker in sufficient detail, so that means we're ready to create our consumer.

Our message processor will consume messages from the topic in much the same way as our Resque workers consumed jobs from a queue, so they will look similar. Let's start by creating a new location for our processor.

```
$ mkdir app/processors
```

TorqueBox will look for message processors in this directory by default, but they can be added anywhere on the load path.

Next, we need to create an app/processors/analytics_processor.rb file and give it the following contents:

TorqueBox/twitalytics/app/processors/analytics_processor.rb
```
class AnalyticsProcessor < TorqueBox::Messaging::MessageProcessor
  def on_message(body)
    # receive messages from broker
  end
end
```

The on_message(body) method of our processor will be invoked by the broker each time a new message is published and pass the JSON message we created earlier as the body argument. The AnalyticsProcessor will do essentially the same job as the UpdateAnalytics Resque task, so we can fill in the on_message(body) method with code that is similar to the UpdateAnalytics.perform(statuses) method.

---

4.   http://torquebox.org/documentation/2.0.2/messaging.html#message-encodings

TorqueBox/twitalytics/app/processors/analytics_processor.rb
```
def on_message(body)
  statuses = JSON.parse(body).map  do |s|
    status = Status.find(s['id'])
    status.preprocess!
    status
  end
  Analytics.refresh(statuses)
end
```

The details of this method are not important to JRuby deployment in general (the Analytics.refresh(statuses) will calculate some Pearson Correlation and Standard Deviation values). But it is important to understand that calculations like these could take more than a few seconds, and that's why we want them to run asynchronously.

Finally, we need to configure the message processor in our config/torquebox.rb file to be a consumer of our topic.

```
topic "/topics/statuses" do
  processor AnalyticsProcessor
end
```

Now we can test it by deploying Twitalytics to the running server. After the application boots up, we'll see this in the console each time a new set of tweets is published:

```
21:13:35,300 INFO  [stdout] ... Updating analytics
```

Our analytics engine is running in the background using TorqueBox's messaging subsystem! We've created a producer that sends messages to a consumer through a destination, as illustrated in Figure 25, *Message flow to the analytics engine*, on page 126.

A message processor requires us to write quite a bit more code than we did with the Backgroundable methods. But we'll take advantage of this extra effort in the next section by pushing messages from the topic to the user interface.

6.8 Pushing to the Browser with Stomplets

TorqueBox provides a Ruby API for Stomplets, which are classes that facilitate bidirectional communication between a server and a client. That means we can send messages from a Stomplet to a web browser that has already loaded a page, as illustrated in Figure 26, *Architecture using Stomplets for asynchronous messaging*, on page 126.

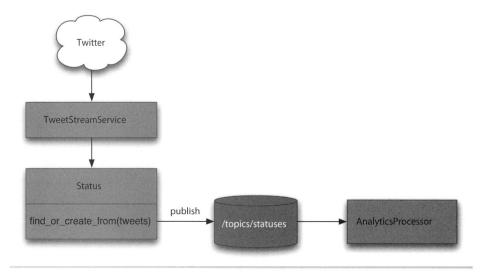

Figure 25—Message flow to the analytics engine

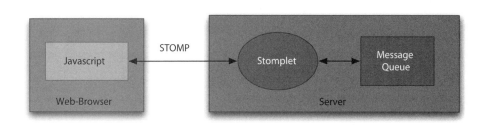

Figure 26— Architecture using Stomplets for asynchronous messaging

The Customer page of Twitalytics provides a good use case for Stomplets. The existing view displays a static list of tweets that is updated only when the page is refreshed. It would be better if the page displayed a live feed, which would require that tweets be pushed to the browser from the server.

Let's create a Stomplet that pushes tweets to any browser that has the Customer page open. To start, we'll need to make Twitalytics Stomplet-ready. This requires a few small additions to our project.

First, we'll inject the TorqueBox::Stomp::StompJavascriptClientProvider Rack middleware into our stack. Open the config.ru, and add these statements right before the run() call:

TorqueBox/twitalytics/config.ru
```
require 'torquebox-stomp'
use TorqueBox::Stomp::StompJavascriptClientProvider
```

The middleware contains the JavaScript that's needed for our web pages to communicate with the Stomplets on the server.

Next, we need to configure the STOMP server. Stomplets communicate with the browser using the Stream-Oriented Messaging Protocol (STOMP), so they need a STOMP server just like our Rails controllers need an HTTP server. The STOMP server will run within the same process as the rest of our application, but it will use a different protocol and port than our HTTP server. Add the following code to the configure() block in the config/torquebox.rb file:

TorqueBox/twitalytics/config/torquebox.rb
```
stomp do
  host 'localhost'
end
```

We also need to explicitly require the torquebox-stomp gem. It was included in our dependencies by the torquebox gem, but it isn't loaded by default because it can cause problems if our code is running outside of the TorqueBox server (we'll cover this in more detail in Section 6.9, *Testing a TorqueBox Application*, on page 131). We want to use an initializer file to load it conditionally, so we need to create a config/initializers/stomp.rb file and put following contents in it:

TorqueBox/twitalytics/config/initializers/stomp.rb
```
begin
  require 'torquebox-stomp'
rescue NameError
  # cannot load Java class javax.jms.MessageListener
end
```

Next, we'll add a helper that gives us access to the URL of our STOMP server. Open the app/helpers/application_helper.rb file, and replace its contents with this:

TorqueBox/twitalytics/app/helpers/application_helper.rb
```
module ApplicationHelper
  include TorqueBox::Injectors

  def stomp_url
    inject('stomp-endpoint')
  end
end
```

The stomp_url() method uses TorqueBox's dependency injection mechanism to get the STOMP endpoint from our configuration. We'll use this method later in the section. Next, we need to create a directory to put our Stomplets in.

```
$ mkdir app/stomplets
```

Twitalytics is ready for Stomplets! Let's build one. In the directory we added earlier, create a status_stomplet.rb file, and put the following code in it:

TorqueBox/twitalytics/app/stomplets/status_stomplet.rb

```ruby
class StatusStomplet < TorqueBox::Stomp::JmsStomplet
  def on_subscribe(subscriber)
    topic = destination_for('/topics/statuses', :topic)
    subscribe_to(subscriber, topic)
  end
end
```

The body of the on_subscribe(subscriber) method retrieves a handle to the topic and connects us to it. Once this connection is made, messages that are published to the topic will be forwarded to the browser. Subclassing Torque-Box::Stomp::JmsStomplet is optional, but we're doing it because we need to integrate with the topic we created in *Creating a Message Processor*, on page 121.

The Stomplet API defines five methods that we can implement in our class.

- configure(config) configures the Stomplet with a set of name-value pairs.
- destroy() is called when the Stomplet is destroyed.
- on_subscribe(subscriber) is called when a client subscribes to a receive message from a Stomplet.
- on_unsubscribe(subscriber) is called when a client unsubscribes from a Stomplet.
- on_message(message) is called when a client sends a message to a Stomplet.

Our communication with the browser will be one-directional. We won't be sending messages from the browser to the server, so we need to implement only the on_subscribe(subscriber) method.

Next, we need to configure the Stomplet in our config/torquebox.rb file. Add the following code to the configure() block:

TorqueBox/twitalytics/config/torquebox.rb

```ruby
stomplet StatusStomplet do
  route '/stomp/status'
end
```

This registers our Stomplet with a STOMP route, which is similar to how we connected Rails routes to Rails controllers. In this case, we've routed the '/stomp/status' path to our StatusStomplet, so requests targeting that URI will be forwarded to our Stomplet.

Our server-side Stomplet work is done. Now we need to modify our client code so that it subscribes to the Stomplet. We'll start by including the JavaScript from our Rack middleware to the app/views/layouts/application.html.erb file. Add the following code to the <head> element:

TorqueBox/twitalytics/app/views/layouts/application.html.erb

```erb
<%= yield :head %>
<%= javascript_include_tag "/stilts-stomp.js" %>
```

We'll use the :head tag to provide connection-specific values for each page. Open the app/views/customers/index.html.erb file, and add the following code to the top of it:

TorqueBox/twitalytics/app/views/customers/index.html.erb
```erb
<% content_for :head do %>
  <script type="text/javascript">
    var stompUrl = "<%= stomp_url %>";
  </script>
<% end %>
```

This sets the stompUrl variable in our JavaScript to the value provided by the ApplicationHelper.stomp_url() method we created earlier.

Next, we'll add the JavaScript that subscribes our browser to the Stomplet. Create a app/assets/javascripts/statuses.js file, and add the following code to it:

TorqueBox/twitalytics/app/assets/javascripts/statuses.js
```javascript
$( function() {
  if (stompUrl) {
    var client = Stomp.client(stompUrl);
  }
});
```

The Stomp class is part of the JavaScript from Rack middleware we included earlier. We're using it to create a client based on the stompUrl if it's set.

Now we can connect to the server by adding the following code after the client variable is initialized but still within the guard clause:

TorqueBox/twitalytics/app/assets/javascripts/statuses.js
```javascript
client.connect( null, null, function() {
  client.subscribe( '/stomp/status', function(message) {
    var s = $.parseJSON( message.body );
    $.each(s, function() {
        onNewStatus(this)
    });
  });
});
```

We're passing a callback function to the connect(null, null, function) method that subscribes the client to the Stomplet we defined earlier. Within that callback, we're invoking the subscribe('/stomp/status', function) method and passing it a callback function as well. The function passed to the subscribe('/stomp/status', function) method will be invoked each time a message is sent from the server to the browser.

In the subscription callback, we're parsing the message.body, which will contain the JSON payload we created in *Creating a Message Processor*, on page 121.

Once the JSON is parsed, the function passes each status record to the onNewStatus(status) function, which we have yet to create.

Let's define an onNewStatus(status) function after the call to connect the client.

TorqueBox/twitalytics/app/assets/javascripts/statuses.js
```
var onNewStatus = function(status) {
  $('#statusTable > tbody > tr:first').before(
    '<tr>' +
      '<td>'+status.creator+'</td>' +
      '<td>'+status.created_at+'</td>' +
      '<td>' +
        '<a href="/customers/retweet/'+status.id+'" ' +
          'data-method="post" rel="nofollow">Retweet</a>' +
      '</td>' +
      '<td>'+status.status_text+'</td>' +
    '</tr>');
};
```

This function uses JavaScript to insert a new table row containing the data from our status into the document model.

Our live feed is ready to be tested. Let's deploy it and browse to http://local-host:8080/customers/index. We'll see new tweets stream onto the page without refreshing.

When a tweet is pulled from Twitter by the TwitterStreamService service, a new Status object is created. This causes a message to be published to the /topics/sta-tuses destinations, which has two consumers: AnalyticsProcessor and StatusStomplet. This flow is illustrated below:

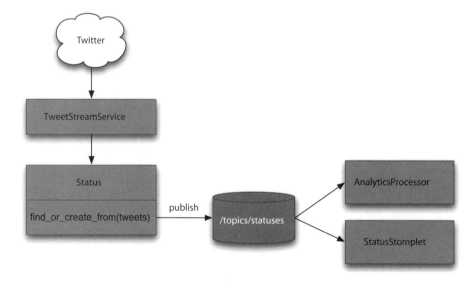

Using the lower-level messaging abstraction instead of the Backgroundable methods required us to write more code, but we're able to do a lot more with our message.

6.9   Testing a TorqueBox Application

An application server decouples our infrastructure from our application. This is generally a good thing, but it can make some traditionally easy things a little more complicated. One of these is testing. Let's run our specs, and you'll see why.

```
$ rpsec spec/
NoMethodError: undefined method `always_background' for #<Class:0x5000cc80>
```

The always_background() method has not been added to the ActiveRecord::Base class. The problem is that we're running outside of the TorqueBox environment, so many of the things we expect to be in place are not. But even if we hacked around and wired up the method, we still wouldn't have background jobs at test time because there is no message queue running! The message queue is a component of the TorqueBox server that is running in another process. Fortunately, there are two testing tools that solve this problem.

TorqueSpec[5] is an integration testing framework that allows you to run Rspec tests within a running TorqueBox server. But it's actually a more inclusive solution than we need to run our specs. Its purpose is to integrate the TorqueBox-based components of our application at test time, but our specs are testing cohesive units of the program. It should be OK to run them independently of each other.

Instead of using TorqueSpec, we'll use the torquebox-no-op gem, which creates stubs of all the TorqueBox methods like always_background() and wires them into our framework. Because the method are stubs, they won't work the way they are supposed to work. But they will allow us to execute the code we are testing.

Let's add this gem to the :test group of our Gemfile:

TorqueBox/twitalytics/Gemfile
```
group :test do
  gem 'rspec-rails'
  gem 'torquebox-no-op', '2.0.2'
end
```

---

5.   https://github.com/torquebox/torquespec

We'll also create a new group for :development and :production to put our other TorqueBox gems in. This will keep them from redefining our stubs at test time.

TorqueBox/twitalytics/Gemfile
```
group :development, :production do
  gem 'torquebox-rake-support', '2.0.2'
  gem 'torquebox', '2.0.2'
end
```

Now we need to run Bundler to install our gems. When it's complete, we can run the specs again.

```
$ rspec spec/
.......

Finished in 3.09 seconds
7 examples, 0 failures
```

Our specs are working! We just need to be careful as we continue to write tests that we don't rely on TorqueBox methods for them to work. But those cases are usually a code smell, anyway. They let us know that we need to break things down into smaller units. But in the event we really do need some TorqueBox infrastructure to test our code, we can always use TorqueSpec.

6.10 Wrapping Up

We made a number of changes to Twitalytics in this chapter. In addition to porting our existing components to TorqueBox, we also created some new components that use the advanced features provided by our new application server. The result is a robust product that runs all of its asynchronous jobs in a single process.

We're using the messaging subsystem to stream live Twitter updates into our application, and the message broker is distributing these updates to multiple consumers. This has allowed us to run our analytics engine asynchronously and push tweets to the browser at the same time.

We've also gained a centralized management console that allows us to inspect and control each of these jobs. This kind of tool is unparalleled in the Ruby market.

We've reached the goal of simplifying our infrastructure, but we've just barely scratched the surface of what TorqueBox can do. One of TorqueBox's key features is its ability to scale. In the next chapter, we'll deploy Twitalytics to a cluster of production servers.

CHAPTER 7

Deploying a TorqueBox Application

TorqueBox runs the gamut of deployment options by supporting traditional deployment tools, deployment as an archive file, and even a built-in web interface for deploying from a Git repository. With TorqueBox, we can choose the deployment strategy that best fits our environment. But which one is right for us?

We'll explore each of the TorqueBox deployment options in this chapter and select the best one for Twitalytics. We'll also define the criteria that should be used when selecting a deployment strategy in any particular environment. Capistrano may be a good fit for one team, but that does not mean it's a good fit for every team.

The criteria we define will ultimately lead us to deploy Twitalytics as a TorqueBox application archive, called a Knob file. This is the fastest, most flexible, and most portable solution for a TorqueBox deployment. In this chapter, we'll create and deploy a Knob file to a dedicated server.

But before we deploy Twitalytics, we'll need to deploy TorqueBox. TorqueBox's defining characteristic as an application server is that it packages all of the components our application needs into a single distribution, which makes it the only piece of infrastructure we need to add to our system. This will simplify our configuration by eliminating the need to install components like Redis and even JRuby.

At the end of the chapter, we'll also deploy a TorqueBox application to the cloud. Unfortunately, the options for cloud deployment of TorqueBox are limited and haven't reached their full potential yet. But the service we'll use is still an improvement over traditional Ruby cloud deployments.

Let's figure out which way of deploying a TorqueBox application is the right one for Twitalytics.

7.1 Choosing a Deployment Strategy

There are three ways in which a TorqueBox application can be deployed, and each method has its own advantages and disadvantages. We can either package and distribute it as a Knob file, push to a directory of loose files with Capistrano, or use Git hooks and the StompBox[1] web application.

Deploying an application as a Knob file is similar to deploying with Warbler. A Knob file is actually a Java archive (JAR) file, which is similar to a WAR file. But a Knob file is specific to TorqueBox, so we can package our entire application into it, not just the web portion.

But deploying as a Knob file might not feel very natural to traditional Ruby programmers who have experience with tools like Capistrano. Capistrano has the advantage of being familiar, but it's far from perfect. It's very opinionated software, which makes it less flexible. Furthermore, its assumptions about deployment make it less portable. For many developers, the appeal of Capistrano is that it integrates with version control software like Git. In these cases, StompBox may be a better and more portable alternative.

StompBox is a deployment application that runs alongside other TorqueBox applications similar to how we deployed BackStage in Chapter 6, *Creating a TorqueBox Application*, on page 103. It has many of the same advantages as using Capistrano, but it works on more platforms, including Windows, and has a web interface. But StompBox is even less flexible since it works only with Git and expects either a post-commit notification or the click of a button in its web interface.

As we select the best method of deployment for our environment, we need to ask ourselves some questions.

What platform will we use?
> If we are deploying to the cloud, we may need to deploy from a Git repository. If we are deploying to a cluster of dedicated servers, we may want to deploy as an archive file so our application can be distributed quickly. Our choice of operating system might also affect our decision because tools like Capistrano will negate the portability provided by TorqueBox and JRuby.

Who are the people on our team?
> If our team has a background with MRI-based Ruby applications, then we'll benefit from traditional deployment techniques that use Capistrano.

---

1. https://github.com/torquebox/stompbox

If our team has a Java background, then using an archive file will be more familiar. But most programmers are good at learning about new technologies, so we shouldn't limit our deployment based on this criteria alone.

What release processes will we use?

Do we need a staging server? Do we need a test server? Do we need a continuous integration (CI) server? These are all important questions in selecting a deployment strategy. They can determine how our application migrates from one environment to the next. If we have a CI server, we can use it to build an archive file that is pushed to our production servers. If we deploy from development to a test environment, then we may want to use Capistrano to ease the deployment of small changes. We can even combine techniques by deploying to a staging environment with Capistrano and then deploying an archive file to production.

In this chapter, we'll be deploying from our development environment to a dedicated production server, which will be simulated by the Vagrant virtual machine we used in the previous chapters. This will drive many of our decisions about how we deploy, but we don't want to lock ourselves into a solution that's specific to this environment.

TorqueBox provides excellent support for Capistrano. Adding just these two lines to our config/deploy.rb would allow us to control the life cycle of our production TorqueBox server and deploy to it:

```
require 'torquebox-capistrano-support'
set :torquebox_home, '/opt/torquebox'
```

But Capistrano is notorious for its poor Windows support, and we want to leverage the portability gained by switching to JRuby, so we won't use Capistrano.

We want a solution that's portable, fast, and repeatable. The strategy that best fits this criteria is Knob file deployment. It will also help us deploy to a cluster of TorqueBox servers in Chapter 8, *Clustering a TorqueBox Application*, on page 149. But before we can create and deploy a Knob file, we need to get our production server ready.

7.2 Creating a Deployment Environment

We need to create a virtual environment to use as a deployment target for Twitalytics. We already prepared the application for TorqueBox in Chapter 6, *Creating a TorqueBox Application*, on page 103, so we're ready to push it to the server. Let's move to our twitalytics directory and use the vagrant command to add a new box from the image we created in Chapter 2, *Creating a Deployment Environment*, on page 19.

```
$ cd ~/code/twitalytics
$ vagrant box add torquebox base-jruby.box
[vagrant] Downloading with Vagrant::Downloaders::File...
[vagrant] Copying box to temporary location...
[vagrant] Extracting box...
[vagrant] Verifying box...
[vagrant] Cleaning up downloaded box...
```

Next, we need to edit our Vagrantfile and adjust the config.vm.box attribute so it points to the newly created torquebox instance.

TorqueBox/twitalytics/Vagrantfile
```
config.vm.box = "torquebox"
```

We also need to forward port 8080 on the guest, which TorqueBox uses, to port 8888 on the host.

TorqueBox/twitalytics/Vagrantfile
```
config.vm.forward_port 8080, 8888
```

Next, we'll increase the memory setting for the virtual machine to 1024MB by adding this statement to the Vagrantfile:

TorqueBox/twitalytics/Vagrantfile
```
config.vm.customize ["modifyvm", :id, "--memory", 1024]
```

Increasing the memory is necessary because TorqueBox is a much heavier platform than the other web servers we've used thus far. If your computer is low on memory, you can probably get away with a value as small as 512MB, but that's not suitable for production.

Our Vagrantfile is ready, but now we need to make some changes to our puppet/manifests/site.pp file before we boot the server.

In Chapter 2, *Creating a Deployment Environment*, on page 19, we provisioned our base image with JRuby. But we won't need this anymore because TorqueBox provides a JRuby runtime for us. We'll discuss this in the next section, but for now we can remove JRuby from our site.pp. The complete recipe should look like this:

TorqueBox/twitalytics/puppet/manifests/site.pp
```
group { "puppet":
    ensure => "present",
}

exec { "apt-update" :
  command => "/usr/bin/apt-get update",
```

```
  require => Group[puppet]
}
Exec["apt-update"] -> Package <| |>

package { "openjdk-6-jdk" :
  ensure => present
}


include apache2
include postgres
include torquebox
```

Our base configuration is ready; let's boot the server.

```
$ vagrant up
[default] Importing base box 'torquebox'...
[default] The guest additions on this VM do not match the install version of
VirtualBox! This may cause things such as forwarded ports, shared
folders, and more to not work properly. If any of those things fail on
this machine, please update the guest additions and repackage the
box.

Guest Additions Version: 4.1.0
VirtualBox Version: 4.1.8
[default] Matching MAC address for NAT networking...
[default] Clearing any previously set forwarded ports...
[default] Forwarding ports...
[default] -- 22 => 2222 (adapter 1)
[default] -- 80 => 8000 (adapter 1)
[default] -- 8080 => 8888 (adapter 1)
[default] Creating shared folders metadata...
[default] Clearing any previously set network interfaces...
[default] Booting VM...
[default] Waiting for VM to boot. This can take a few minutes.
[default] VM booted and ready for use!
[default] Mounting shared folders...
[default] -- v-root: /vagrant
[default] -- manifests: /tmp/vagrant-puppet/manifests
[default] -- v-pp-m0: /tmp/vagrant-puppet/modules-0
[default] Running provisioner: Vagrant::Provisioners::Puppet...
[default] Running Puppet with /tmp/vagrant-puppet/manifests/site.pp...
stdin: is not a tty
notice: /Stage[main]//Exec[apt-update]/returns: executed successfully
notice: /Stage[main]/Postgres/Exec[psql -c "ALTER USER vagrant WITH PASSWORD...
...
[default] notice: Finished catalog run in 43.38 seconds
```

Now that the server is running, we're ready to install our new infrastructure. But TorqueBox is an application server, so it's the only thing we need to add.

7.3   Installing TorqueBox

TorqueBox is distributed as both a gem and a binary file. We installed the gem on our development machines because it allowed us to use our existing JRuby installation. But on our production server, we want to use the JRuby runtime provided by TorqueBox, so we'll install the binary file. The TorqueBox binary distribution includes an embedded JRuby runtime, which simplifies the deployment process and ensures a degree of compatibility between our server and its platform. But that's the only difference between the binary distribution and the gem.

We could install the TorqueBox gem on our production server; it's a perfectly acceptable approach. But in addition to requiring that a JRuby runtime be present, the gem also inserts a layer of abstraction between the TorqueBox installation and how we interact with it. This was helpful in development, but in production we want to interact directly with TorqueBox by adjusting its configuration and manually deploying to it.

Let's begin by creating a TorqueBox module in our Puppet configuration.

```
$ mkdir -p puppet/modules/torquebox/manifests
```

Next, we'll create an init.pp file in the new directory. Open this file, and add the following content to it:

TorqueBox/twitalytics/puppet/modules/torquebox/manifests/init.pp
```
class torquebox {

}
```

This class will contain all of the configuration for our TorqueBox installation. Let's add some resources to it.

We need to define the location where we'll install TorqueBox. Add this variable definition to the torquebox class:

TorqueBox/twitalytics/puppet/modules/torquebox/manifests/init.pp
```
$tb_home = "/opt/torquebox"
$tb_version = "2.0.2"
```

Next, we need to ensure that the unzip package is installed, because TorqueBox is distributed as a zip file. Add this resource to the class:

TorqueBox/twitalytics/puppet/modules/torquebox/manifests/init.pp
```
package { unzip:
  ensure => present
}
```

Now we can download and unzip the TorqueBox binaries by adding the following resource:

```
exec { "download_tb":
  command => "wget -O /tmp/torquebox.zip http://bit.ly/torquebox-2_0_2",
  path => $path,
  creates => "/tmp/torquebox.zip",
  unless => "ls /opt | grep torquebox-${tb_version}",
  require => [Package["openjdk-6-jdk"], User[torquebox]]
}
```

Next, we'll add a resource that unzips the file we just downloaded.

```
exec { "unpack_tb" :
  command => "unzip /tmp/torquebox.zip -d /opt",
  path => $path,
  creates => "${tb_home}-${tb_version}",
  require => [Exec["download_tb"], Package[unzip]]
}
```

We've extracted the zip file into a version-specific directory under /opt. But we also need to define a symlink that points to the current version of TorqueBox by adding this resource:

```
file { $tb_home:
    ensure => link,
    target => "${tb_home}-${tb_version}",
    require => Exec["unpack_tb"]
}
```

Now we're ready to provision our server by reloading the box.

```
$ vagrant reload
[default] Attempting graceful shutdown of VM...
[default] VM already created. Booting if it's not already running...
[default] Clearing any previously set forwarded ports...
[default] Forwarding ports...
[default] -- 22 => 2222 (adapter 1)
[default] -- 80 => 8000 (adapter 1)
[default] -- 8080 => 8888 (adapter 1)
[default] Creating shared folders metadata...
[default] Clearing any previously set network interfaces...
[default] Booting VM...
[default] Waiting for VM to boot. This can take a few minutes.
[default] VM booted and ready for use!
[default] Mounting shared folders...
[default] -- v-root: /vagrant
[default] -- manifests: /tmp/vagrant-puppet/manifests
```

```
[default] -- v-pp-m0: /tmp/vagrant-puppet/modules-0
[default] Running provisioner: Vagrant::Provisioners::Puppet...
[default] Running Puppet with /tmp/vagrant-puppet/manifests/site.pp...
stdin: is not a tty
notice: /Stage[main]//Exec[apt-update]/returns: executed successfully
notice: /Stage[main]/Postgres/Exec[psql -c "ALTER USER vagrant WITH PASSWORD ...
notice: /Stage[main]/Torquebox/User[torquebox]/ensure: created
notice: /Stage[main]/Torquebox/Exec[copy_ssh_key]/returns: executed successfully
notice: /Stage[main]/Torquebox/Package[unzip]/ensure: ensure changed 'purged'...
notice: /Stage[main]/Torquebox/Exec[download_tb]/returns: executed successfully
notice: /Stage[main]/Torquebox/Exec[unpack_tb]/returns: executed successfully
notice: /Stage[main]/Torquebox/File[/opt/torquebox]/ensure: created
notice: Finished catalog run in 273.57 seconds
```

TorqueBox is installed, but it's not running yet. Let's log into the box with
the vagrant ssh command and take a closer look at what we've done.

```
vagrant@lucid64:~$ ls /opt/torquebox
jboss  jruby  Rakefile  share
```

The installation contains three directories and a Rake script. The jboss directory contains all of the underlying infrastructure for the JBoss server that
TorqueBox is built on. The jruby directory contains the JRuby runtime that
TorqueBox will use to execute our application. The share directory contains
some scripts and configuration files (including the stilts-stomp.js file we imported
in the previous chapter). The Rake script contains tasks that we can use to
control the life cycle of the server. We can get a list of them by running the
following command:

```
vagrant@lucid64:~$ cd /opt/torquebox && jruby/bin/jruby -S rake --tasks
(in /opt/torquebox-2.0.2)
rake torquebox:check             # Check your installation of the TorqueBox ...
rake torquebox:launchd:check     # Check if TorqueBox is installed as a laun...
rake torquebox:launchd:install   # Install TorqueBox as an launchd daemon
rake torquebox:launchd:restart   # Restart TorqueBox when running as an laun...
rake torquebox:launchd:start     # Start TorqueBox when running as a launchd...
rake torquebox:launchd:stop      # Stop TorqueBox when running as an launchd...
rake torquebox:run               # Run TorqueBox server
rake torquebox:upstart:check     # Check if TorqueBox is installed as an ups...
rake torquebox:upstart:install   # Install TorqueBox as an upstart service
rake torquebox:upstart:restart   # Restart TorqueBox when running as an upst...
rake torquebox:upstart:start     # Start TorqueBox when running as an upstar...
rake torquebox:upstart:stop      # Stop TorqueBox when running as an upstart...
```

The torquebox:launchd tasks are used to install TorqueBox as a service on Mac
OS X systems, so they won't be useful in this example. But the torquebox:upstart
tasks can be used to install TorqueBox as an init service on Linux systems.
We'll add these to our Puppet configuration.

Close the connection to the virtual machine with the exit command, and we'll return to the twitalytics directory on our host. Now we can edit the puppet/modules/torquebox/manifests/init.pp file again and add this resource to the torquebox class.

TorqueBox/twitalytics/puppet/modules/torquebox/manifests/init.pp
```
user { "torquebox":
  ensure => present,
  managehome => true,
  system => true
}
```

The upstart tasks require that a torquebox user be present on the system so it can run the server process as this user. In addition to creating the account, we also need to change the privileges on the TorqueBox home directory by making the torquebox user its owner.

TorqueBox/twitalytics/puppet/modules/torquebox/manifests/init.pp
```
exec { "chown_tb_home":
    command => "chown -RH torquebox:torquebox ${tb_home}",
    path => $path,
    require => [File[$tb_home], User[torquebox]]
}
```

In a little while, we'll be logging in as this user with SSH, so we'll need to create a public key for it. To make things easier, we'll copy the existing key from the vagrant user's home directory (we should use the ssh-keygen tool to generate a new key for each user, but this will save us some time in working through the example).

TorqueBox/twitalytics/puppet/modules/torquebox/manifests/init.pp
```
exec { copy_ssh_key :
  command => "cp -R /home/vagrant/.ssh /home/torquebox/.ssh",
  path => $path,
  creates => "/home/torquebox/.ssh",
  require => User[torquebox]
}

file { "/home/torquebox/.ssh":
  ensure => directory,
  owner => torquebox,
  group => torquebox,
  recurse => true,
  require => Exec[copy_ssh_key]
}
```

This will copy the /home/vagrant/.ssh directory and apply the new permissions recursively.

Now we're ready to add a resource that invokes the torquebox:upstart:install task.

TorqueBox/twitalytics/puppet/modules/torquebox/manifests/init.pp

```
exec { "upstart_install":
    cwd => $tb_home,
    command => "${tb_home}/jruby/bin/jruby -S rake torquebox:upstart:install",
    environment => ["JBOSS_HOME=${tb_home}/jboss", "TORQUEBOX_HOME=${tb_home}",
                    'SERVER_OPTS="-b=0.0.0.0"'],
    creates => "/etc/init/torquebox.conf",
    require => [File[$tb_home], User["torquebox"]]
}
```

This task creates the /etc/init/torquebox.conf file on the server with the configuration for our service. In addition to setting the JBOSS_HOME and TORQUEBOX_HOME environment variables, we've also set the SERVER_OPTS variable to -b=0.0.0.0. This will bind the server to the *default route*, which will allow us to view it from the host browser.

Next, we'll ensure that the service is started by adding the following resource:

TorqueBox/twitalytics/puppet/modules/torquebox/manifests/init.pp

```
exec { "upstart_start":
    cwd => $tb_home,
    command => "${tb_home}/jruby/bin/jruby -S rake torquebox:upstart:start",
    environment => ["JBOSS_HOME=${tb_home}/jboss", "TORQUEBOX_HOME=${tb_home}"],
    require => Exec["upstart_install"]
}
```

Now we're ready to provision the server again.

```
$ vagrant provision
[default] Running provisioner: Vagrant::Provisioners::Puppet...
[default] Running Puppet with /tmp/vagrant-puppet/manifests/site.pp...
stdin: is not a tty
notice: /Stage[main]//Exec[apt-update]/returns: executed successfully
notice: /Stage[main]/Postgres/Exec[psql -c "ALTER USER vagrant WITH PASSWORD ...
notice: /Stage[main]/Torquebox/Exec[chown_tb_home]/returns: executed successf...
notice: /Stage[main]/Torquebox/Exec[upstart_install]/returns: executed succes...
notice: /Stage[main]/Torquebox/Exec[upstart_start]/returns: executed successf...
notice: Finished catalog run in 12.34 seconds
```

TorqueBox is installed and running. Let's deploy our application to it.

7.4 Deploying an Archive File

We decided earlier in the chapter that deploying Twitalytics as a Knob file is the best strategy for our environment. It will give us most of the advantages that Warbler gave us in Chapter 3, *Deploying an Archive File*, on page 37, but it also solves many of the problems Warbler created.

We can package Twitalytics into a Knob archive with the torquebox:archive task. We'll run it with the exclude option to keep it from packing our virtual machine and development database.

```
$ rake torquebox:archive exclude=puppet,.box,.war,.sqlite3
Creating archive: twitalytics.knob
added manifest
...
Created archive: ~/code/twitalytics/twitalytics.knob
```

Knob files use the .knob extension, but they are really just JAR files. This makes them similar to the WAR file we created with Warbler. But WAR files cater to Java-based servers. We can do much more with Knob files because they are specific to TorqueBox. With Warbler, there was not a good way of incorporating our background Resque workers into the archive. A Knob file can contain all of the code for our TorqueBox subsystems, including messaging, services, and jobs.

Warbler also made it difficult to have a development environment that was similar to our production environment. If we ran a servlet container in development, we lost the instant feedback that's expected in a Rails application. We had to either deploy each time we made a change or run WEBrick.

TorqueBox can handle both archive files and a directory of loose source code files, which gives us instant feedback in development by running the server against the project directory on the filesystem (as we did in Chapter 6, *Creating a TorqueBox Application*, on page 103). But we can also deploy to an identical container in production. We get the best of both worlds this way.

Now that we've created an archive file, we have a self-contained bundle that can be distributed however we'd like. Knob files are completely portable; they don't require SSH, Git, or any other specific technology. We only need to place them in the TorqueBox home directory of our production server.

We'll use a tool called torquebox-remote-deployer[2] to move the Twitalytics Knob file onto our Vagrant box. It provides a few Rake tasks that simplify the deployment process. We'll start by adding it as a dependency to our project's Gemfile.

TorqueBox/twitalytics/Gemfile
```
gem 'torquebox-remote-deployer', '0.1.1'
```

After we run Bundler's install command, we'll have some new Rake tasks available to us.

---

2.   https://github.com/jkutner/torquebox-remote-deployer

```
$ rake --tasks
...
rake torquebox:remote:deploy          # Deploy the archive file to the remot...
rake torquebox:remote:exec[cmd]       # Execute Ruby commands against the re...
rake torquebox:remote:stage           # Upload the archive file to the remot...
rake torquebox:remote:undeploy        # Undeploy the archive file to the rem...
```

To use these tasks, we need to create a config/torquebox_remote.rb file. We'll use this file to configure how the deployer connects to our remote server. Let's edit the file and add the following code to it:

TorqueBox/twitalytics/config/torquebox_remote.rb
```
TorqueBox::RemoteDeploy.configure do
  torquebox_home "/opt/torquebox"
  hostname "localhost"
  port "2222"
  user "torquebox"
  key "~/.vagrant.d/insecure_private_key"
end
```

We set the torquebox_home attribute to the location that we extracted the zip file with our Puppet scripts. The rest of the configuration is similar to how we connected to the server with our vagrant ssh command, except that we're using the torquebox user instead of the vagrant user. That's why we copied the public key.

Before we use the deployer, we need to configure Bundler for deployment by running this command:

```
$ bundle install --deployment
```

This will copy all of our gem dependencies into the vendor/bundle directory. When the Knob file is created, it will package this directory with the rest of our application in the same way that Warbler packaged our gems into the WAR file in Chapter 1, *Getting Started with JRuby*, on page 1. Having the gems in our archive file ensures that we are running the same code in every location we deploy to. There will be no need to run bundle install on the production server and thus no chance of downloading a gem that is corrupted or has been tampered with.

Now let's invoke the torquebox:remote:stage task, which will rebuild our archive and push it to the server.

```
$ rake torquebox:remote:stage exclude=puppet,.box,.war,.sqlite3
Creating archive: twitalytics.knob
...
Copying twitalytics.knob: 474925/474925
```

This stages the Knob file by copying it to the server but does not actually deploy it. This step is important because we need to run our migrations before starting the application. Since we'll be repeating this each time we deploy, we'll put it in a lib/tasks/deploy.rake script with a single task that will do everything. Create that file, and add the following code to it:

TorqueBox/twitalytics/lib/tasks/deploy.rake

```
namespace :deploy do
  task :knob do
    ENV["exclude"] = "puppet,.box,.war,.sqlite3"
    Rake::Task["torquebox:remote:stage"].invoke
  end
end
```

The deploy task will do exactly what the torquebox:remote:stage earlier did. Let's try it.

```
$ rake deploy:knob
Creating archive: twitalytics.knob
...
Copying twitalytics.knob: 474925/474925
```

The Knob file has been copied to the server. Now we need to invoke a task that runs our migrations. Add the following code after the previous invocation:

TorqueBox/twitalytics/lib/tasks/deploy.rake

```
Rake::Task["torquebox:remote:exec"].
  invoke("bundle exec rake db:migrate")
puts "Migrations Complete..."
```

This will ensure that the production database schema is up-to-date. The bundle exec command will run the Rake task within the context of the gems we packaged into the Knob file earlier. Let's run the process again to test it:

```
$ rake deploy:knob
Creating archive: twitalytics.knob
...
Copying twitalytics.knob: 474925/474925
==  CreateStatuses: migrating =================================================
-- create_table(:statuses)
   -> 0.0040s
   -> 0 rows
==  CreateStatuses: migrated (0.0060s) =======================================

==  CreateAnalytics: migrating ===============================================
-- create_table(:analytics)
   -> 0.0040s
   -> 1 rows
==  CreateAnalytics: migrated (0.0040s) ======================================
Migrations Complete...
```

Deploying TorqueBox to the Cloud

TorqueBox can be run in the cloud using Red Hat's OpenShift cloud service.[a] Open-Shift provides two cloud solutions: Express and Flex. OpenShift Express is a free service with some memory and feature constraints. OpenShift Flex is more fully featured but is not free. Unfortunately, TorqueBox is supported only on the Express platform as of this writing.

Despite the memory constraints, OpenShift still supports powerful TorqueBox features such as background jobs, caching, and messaging. But it does not yet support STOMP or clustering. Even with these limitations, running TorqueBox on OpenShift provides many advantages over a traditional Ruby deployment. We can still integrate the scheduler and long-running services with the rest of our application, and our ability to grow to meet increased demand will improve.

We won't try deploying Twitalytics to the cloud because we would need to remove our Stomplet and tweak some other configuration. Furthermore, the OpenShift support for TorqueBox is fairly new and subject to change, but some excellent resources on the Web describe how it can be done.[b]

As TorqueBox and OpenShift mature, they will become the most robust and scalable cloud-based platform for a JRuby application.

a.   https://openshift.redhat.com/
b.   http://torquebox.org/news/2012/03/28/torquebox-openshift/

The task rebuilt the Knob file, copied it to the server, and migrated the database. Now we can deploy the Knob file that is already on the server to the running TorqueBox instance. We'll do this by adding the following invocation to the deploy:knob block:

TorqueBox/twitalytics/lib/tasks/deploy.rake
```
Rake::Task["torquebox:remote:stage:deploy"].invoke
```

Let's run our task one last time.

```
$ rake deploy:knob
Creating archive: twitalytics.knob
...
Copying twitalytics.knob: 474925/474925
Migrations Complete...
Deployment Complete!
```

The process ran a tad faster because the migrations did not need to make any changes to our schema. The application will take a few seconds to start up, and we can check its progress by logging into the Vagrant box with vagrant ssh and running this command to view the log file:

```
vagrant@lucid64:~$ tail -f /opt/torquebox/jboss/standalone/log/server.log
```

When we see the following message in the log, we'll know it's ready:

```
10:47:04,693 INFO  [org.jboss.as.server] (DeploymentScanner-threads - 2) JBAS018
559: Deployed "twitalytics-knob.yml"
```

The next time we need to deploy, we can run `rake deploy:knob` again, and TorqueBox will hot-deploy our application. This is not the same as zero-downtime deployment, however. Hot deployment loads a new version of our application without shutting down the server process, but there is still a short gap where requests can be missed. This should be sufficient for most applications because the overhead of deploying an application is much lower than restarting and entire server, so it happens relatively quickly. In Chapter 8, *Clustering a TorqueBox Application*, on page 149, we'll use a proxy that can handle zero-downtime deployment for us when running in a cluster.

Now we can exit the virtual machine and point a browser to http://localhost:8888, where we'll see the application running. That means our deployment was successful. Let's commit our changes to the repository.

```
$ git add .
$ git commit -m "added torquebox deployment script"
```

Finally, let's return our Bundler configuration to its nondeployment state by running this command:

```
$ bundle install --no-deployment
```

One of the advantages of a Knob file is that we can distribute it in many different ways. We've deployed Twitalytics directly to our production machine from development, but we could have built it on a continuous integration server and pushed it only after our integration tests pass. We could also store it on a service like Amazon S3[3] and have our Puppet scripts pull it when the server is ready for maintenance. Packaging our application into a single neat and tidy file makes our deployment process extremely flexible.

7.5 Wrapping Up

TorqueBox has immensely simplified our infrastructure. With this single software package, we are able to run recurring jobs, background jobs, and long-running jobs in the same runtime. We didn't even need to install JRuby! But TorqueBox's biggest contribution is our simplified deployment strategy.

We chose to deploy Twitalytics as a Knob file because it gave us all the benefits of archive file deployment without the headaches of Warbler. TorqueBox

---

3.   http://aws.amazon.com/s3/

provides support for other tools, such as Capistrano and Git hooks. But archive file deployment is best suited for our environment because it's fast, portable, repeatable, and dependable.

In the next chapter, you'll learn how deploying our application as a Knob file will improve its ability to scale. We'll create a cluster of TorqueBox servers and push this single file to all of them in one step.

CHAPTER 8

Clustering a TorqueBox Application

TorqueBox's most powerful feature is scalability, which is something Ruby applications have traditionally struggled with. TorqueBox is different because of its built-in mechanisms that allow a group of distributed servers to communicate and coordinate with each other. We can leverage these communication paths to build applications that become smarter when deployed to a cluster.

A cluster is set of connected computers that work together as a single system. Each computer in the cluster is referred to as a *node*, and the degree to which these nodes are connected depends on the cluster's topology. A topology describes the different communication paths between nodes and determines how each node communicates (or does not communicate) with the other nodes.

In its simplest form, a cluster could include a set of distributed Mongrel instances that are load balanced by an HTTP server like Apache. But without any interconnections between the Mongrel nodes, the cluster doesn't have much power.

To increase the communication between nodes, most clusters introduce shared storage like a SQL database, Redis (with Resque), and Memcache. But these frameworks add more components to an already complicated infrastructure. With TorqueBox, we can create a cluster that has all the capabilities of a complex topology like this, without the infrastructure headaches.

A TorqueBox cluster provides many levels of communication between nodes, which allows it to scale unlike any other Ruby platform. In this chapter, we'll create a TorqueBox cluster like the one pictured in Figure 27, *Levels of communication in a TorqueBox cluster*, on page 150 that leverages session replication

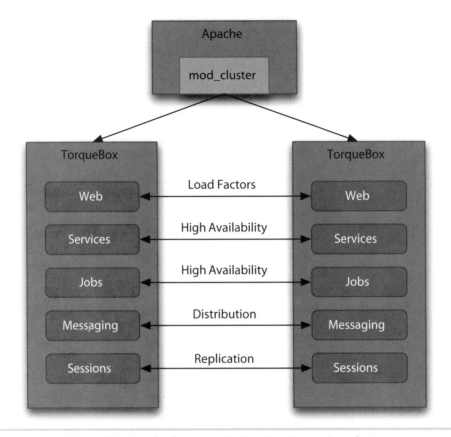

Figure 27—Levels of communication in a TorqueBox cluster

and high-availability jobs to increase its processing power and uptime. These features will help us avoid common clustering problems.

Without TorqueBox, a cluster may introduce concerns that did not exist when the application was a single instance. As an example, consider a website with a shopping cart that is stored in a user's session. When users add something to their cart, they expect it to be there even if their requests are redirected to another node in the cluster. It's common to solve this problem by storing the session data in a SQL database. But that can slow down the entire site if constant session access interferes with the database's normal activities. Another solution is to use an object caching system like Memcache.[1] But Memcache adds additional infrastructure, such as Redis and the SQL database, that has to be managed and monitored.

---

1.   http://memcached.org/

TorqueBox solves the distributed session problem with a built-in storage mechanism called a *data grid*. This grid, which is powered by Infinispan,[2] can replicate itself across the cluster without the need for additional infrastructure. In this chapter, we'll enhance Twitalytics to use this clusterable storage mechanism for its user sessions. We'll also coordinate our background jobs so they won't duplicate each other as we stand up new nodes in the cluster.

But before we use these new TorqueBox features, we'll need to set up a cluster.

8.1 Creating the Cluster

We're going to simulate a TorqueBox cluster by running multiple instances of the server on the same machine. We could run TorqueBox on a cluster of Vagrant boxes, but not all computers can handle that kind of load. Furthermore, the networking bridge of the virtual machine and the increase in the communication demands of TorqueBox do not play well together on all platforms. To demonstrate TorqueBox's clustering in a way that works on all kinds of hardware and operating systems, we'll run the two TorqueBox instances on our development machine.

Before we get started, let's remove all of our earlier deployments (this isn't completely necessary, but it will ensure that you see the same output as described in this chapter). The quick and dirty way to do this is with the following command:

```
$ rm -rf `torquebox env torquebox_home`/jboss/standalone/deployments/*
```

Now we're ready to boot our cluster. We can start the first server by using the same torquebox run command we used in the previous chapters, but we'll add two options.

```
$ torquebox run --clustered -b <ip-address>
```

The --clustered option initializes a few extra components that use the multicast channel to discover and be discovered by other nodes. The -b option binds the instance to an IP address. You'll have to replace *<ip-address>* with the actual address of your network interface.

To start our second node, we need to open a new terminal and run the following command, which is similar to the previous command but with some additional JBoss options (replace *<ip-address>* with your actual IP address again):

---

2.   http://www.jboss.org/infinispan

Joe asks:

What Is Multicast?

Multicast is a routing protocol for sending IP packets to multiple receivers in a single transmission. It is most commonly used for streaming video and music across the Internet, but it's an excellent solution for clusters where a node needs to communicate with all other nodes at the same time.

The nodes in our TorqueBox cluster are listening to a multicast address, which must be in the range of 224.0.0.0 through 239.255.255.255 (TorqueBox uses 230.0.0.4 by default). When a new node starts up, it sends a message to this address that notifies the other nodes of its presence. This allows the cluster to scale dynamically because the addresses of other nodes do not have to be predefined.

```
$ torquebox run --clustered -b <ip-address> --node-name=node2 \
        --data-directory=/tmp/node2 --port-offset=100
```

We gave this server a distinct node name and its own temporary directory with the --data-directory option. This will prevent it from conflicting with the first node.[3] We're also offsetting the ports it will use. TorqueBox listens on several ports, including 8080 for HTTP traffic, 8443 for HTTPS, 8675 for STOMP, and 5445 for messaging. But only one of our servers will be able to bind to each of these. The --port-offset options allows the second server to have a distinct set of ports.

When the second node is started, we'll see the following output in the console of both nodes:

```
13:19:55,229 INFO [org.hornetq.core.server.cluster.impl.BridgeImpl]
(Thread-1 (group:HornetQ-server-threads1087933741-133488826)) Connecting
bridge sf.default-cluster-connection.59237021-4398-11e1-908b-0a0027000000
to its destination
[4dad9355-3b32-11e1-96d7-c82a144c0ae1]
13:19:55,340 INFO [org.hornetq.core.server.cluster.impl.BridgeImpl]
(Thread-1 (group:HornetQ-server-threads1087933741-133488826)) Bridge
sf.default-cluster-connection.59237021-4398-11e1-908b-0a0027000000 is
connected [4dad9355-3b32-11e1-96d7-c82a144c0ae1-> sf.default-cluster-
connection.59237021-4398-11e1-908b-0a0027000000]
```

This lets us know that the nodes have bridged their messaging subsystems, which means that TorqueBox is now providing automatic web session replication, distributed caching, load balancing of messages, and intelligent distribution of background jobs.

---

3.   https://issues.jboss.org/browse/AS7-2493

In the following sections, we'll enhance Twitalytics to use these features. But first, we need to put a proxy in front of our cluster so that web requests can be distributed across it.

8.2 Installing the Apache Cluster Module

We're going to proxy our cluster with the Apache HTTP Server and the JBoss mod_cluster module.[4] This module will forward requests from Apache to one of the cluster nodes behind it and balance the load that each node receives. Unlike other Apache balancing modules, mod_cluster leverages an additional communication link that transmits life-cycle events and balancing factors from the nodes to the proxy. This allows the module to make more informed decisions about where to send each request.

Let's start by downloading the mod_cluster binaries from the official website.[5] There are packages for just about every platform (including Windows), but the following examples will reference the Mac OS X package. The steps for other platforms will be essentially the same.

Once the binary package is downloaded, put it in your home directory and extract it with this command:

```
$ tar xvzf mod_cluster-1.2.0.Final-macosx-x86-ssl.tar.gz
```

This will create a opt/jboss directory, which includes a complete Apache HTTP Server. We'll use this server as our proxy, but we need to configure the server so that it can run from our home directory. We can do this by running the following command:

```
$ ./opt/jboss/httpd/sbin/installhome.sh

Running : installhome.sh : 2010-05-04 18:26:40 +0200 (Tue, 04 May 2010) $

Installing in ~/opt/jboss/httpd
~/opt/jboss/httpd/sbin/apachectl
~/opt/jboss/httpd/httpd/conf/httpd.conf
~/opt/jboss/httpd/sbin/envvars
~/opt/jboss/httpd/sbin/apxs
~/opt/jboss/httpd/htdocs/build/config_vars.mk
```

On Windows, we would need to run the httpd-2.2\bin\installconf.bat file instead.

Now we can start the Apache HTTP Server by running the apachectl command:

---

4. http://www.jboss.org/mod_cluster
5. http://www.jboss.org/mod_cluster/downloads/1-1-3

```
$ ./opt/jboss/httpd/sbin/apachectl start
httpd: Could not reliably determine the server's fully qualified domain name...
```

The proxy is running. We can verify this by pointing a browser to http://local-host:8000, where we'll see the "It works!" splash page. Because we are running from our home directory (and not as the root user), the server is listening on port 8000 instead of 80.

Next, ensure that the TorqueBox servers we started earlier in the chapter are still running. If they are, then they have already registered themselves with the proxy. There is no additional configuration needed. We can see Twitlaytics by browsing to http://localhost:8000/dashboard/index (the default Apache index page hasn't been routed to our application's root).

The nodes in our cluster are communicating with the Mod-Cluster Management Protocol (MCMP) on port 6666. The server also provides a web interface on this port that allows us to view the status of this communication. We can see it by pointing a browser to http://localhost:6666/mod_cluster_manager. Unfortunately, many browsers will block this port by default, so we may encounter an error with the message "Not allowed to use restricted network port." Getting around this error depends on the browser and system being used. For Chrome on Mac OS X, we can start the browser with this command:

```
$ open /Applications/Google\ Chrome.app --args --explicitly-allowed-ports=6666
```

Because the mod_cluster-manager page contains simple HTML, it may also be sufficient to use a tool like curl or wget to view its contents.

If you are able to view the manager, you'll see that the servers running have registered themselves as nodes in the cluster, as pictured in Figure 28, *The mod_cluster-manager web interface*, on page 155. They are also using the AJP protocol to connect to the proxy, which we discussed when we used it to connect Trinidad and Apache in Chapter 5, *Deploying a Trinidad Application*, on page 75.

Our cluster is ready. We've set it up locally by running two servers on the same host, but the steps would be mostly the same if we were running on a LAN with multicast support. It's still possible to set up a cluster without multicast enabled, but it's not as configuration-free. We would have to explicitly tell each server where the other nodes are located. This is most commonly needed in a cloud environment such as Amazon's EC2.[6]

Next, let's deploy Twitalytics to our cluster.

---

6.   http://aws.amazon.com/vpc/faqs/#R4

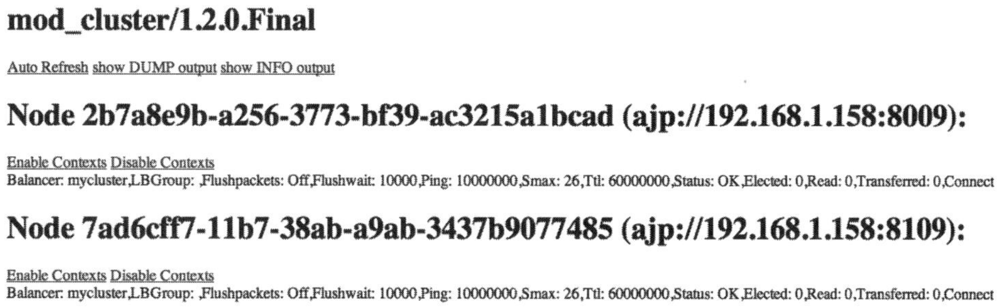

mod_cluster/1.2.0.Final

Auto Refresh show DUMP output show INFO output

Node 2b7a8e9b-a256-3773-bf39-ac3215a1bcad (ajp://192.168.1.158:8009):

Enable Contexts Disable Contexts
Balancer: mycluster,LBGroup: ,Flushpackets: Off,Flushwait: 10000,Ping: 10000000,Smax: 26,Ttl: 60000000,Status: OK ,Elected: 0,Read: 0,Transferred: 0,Connect

Node 7ad6cff7-11b7-38ab-a9ab-3437b9077485 (ajp://192.168.1.158:8109):

Enable Contexts Disable Contexts
Balancer: mycluster,LBGroup: ,Flushpackets: Off,Flushwait: 10000,Ping: 10000000,Smax: 26,Ttl: 60000000,Status: OK ,Elected: 0,Read: 0,Transferred: 0,Connect

Figure 28—The mod_cluster-manager web interface

8.3 Deploying to the Cluster

Deploying to a cluster isn't much different from deploying to a single TorqueBox instance. The torquebox-remote-deployer gem can help us with remote cluster deployments, but our cluster nodes are running locally and have access to the same filesystem, so we won't use the gem.

We can deploy to both TorqueBox instances with the torquebox deploy command, as we did in Chapter 6, *Creating a TorqueBox Application*, on page 103. Be sure you return to the ~/code/twitalytics directory that contains our application code and run the following command:

```
$ torquebox deploy
Deployed: twitalytics-knob.yml
  into: ~/.rvm/gems/jruby-1.6.7/gems/torquebox-server-2.0.2-java/jboss...
```

Because these nodes are sharing the same TorqueBox home directory, the deployment will be picked up by both of them. Let's test this by pointing one browser to http://<ip-address>:8080 and another browser to http://<ip-address>:8180, where *<ip-address>* should be replaced by the IP address you passed to the torquebox command. The 8180 port in the second URL is the offset HTTP port of the second TorqueBox node. We'll see Twitalytics running in both places.

We've deployed our application to the cluster, but we aren't making the most of it yet. Let's enhance Twitalytics so that each node interacts with the other nodes.

8.4 Using High-Availability Jobs and Services

Nodes in a TorqueBox cluster have the ability to communicate with each other, which is important when an application needs to retain session state or when background jobs need to coordinate with other background jobs.

The most common case is when two jobs need to coordinate so that they do not perform duplicate tasks.

For example, you may have noticed that both of our TorqueBox instances are logging this statement to the console:

```
14:35:11,414 INFO  [stdout] (JobScheduler$twitalytics-knob.yml_Worker-1) No
statuses have been deleted.
```

This means that both of our instances are running the recurring DeleteOldStatuses job. But it's necessary for only one of our nodes to run this job because they are both accessing the same database. In this example, it's unlikely that anything bad would happen because of the job being duplicated, but there are many cases where it could.

We need to modify this job's configuration so that it runs on only one node. A naive approach to doing this might involve a custom configuration for each node. But this would be fragile and difficult to maintain. Furthermore, it would not protect against the very likely case that the node running the job crashes or is shut down; the cluster would no longer have a node that can run the job.

With TorqueBox, we can configure the job to be a high-availability singleton, which means that the nodes in the cluster will coordinate with each other to ensure that only one instance of the job is run at a time. But if the node that is running the job crashes, another node will start running the job in its place.

The communication needed to establish a singleton in our cluster has already started without us even configuring anything. You may have noticed this in the console output of one of the TorqueBox servers.

```
14:33:24,099 INFO  [org.projectodd.polyglot.hasingleton] (AsynchViewChangeHandl
er Thread) Becoming HASingleton master.
14:33:24,112 INFO  [org.projectodd.polyglot.hasingleton] (AsynchViewChangeHandl
er Thread) inquire if we should be master
```

The node that logged these statements detected that another node with the same application was started. It then determined that it should become the master node and notified the other nodes of its role. This is good, but we still need to configure our job so it leverages this link. Let's open the config/torquebox.rb file and find the configuration for our DeleteOldStatuses job. We'll add a statement that sets the singleton attribute to true like this:

TorqueBox/cluster/config/torquebox.rb
```
job DeleteOldStatuses do
  cron "0 0/5 * * * ?"
  singleton true
```

```
config do
  max_age 30
end
end
```

Now we can deploy the application again with the torquebox command.

```
$ torquebox deploy
```

After both nodes boot Twitalytics, we'll find that the cleanup job is running on only one of them (the node that claimed the HASingleton master role).

Next, let's kill the master node by pressing Ctrl+C in the console of the server running the job. After doing so, we should see that the other node picks up the role of master and starts logging the following statement to the console:

```
14:55:11,414 INFO  [stdout] (JobScheduler$twitalytics-knob.yml_Worker-1) No
statuses have been deleted.
```

Our singleton job is working! Before we move on, be sure to restart the node we killed.

In addition to scheduled jobs, we can also configure long-running TorqueBox services as singletons. This will be useful in the case of the TwitterStreamService, which we do not want to run on more than one node because it could cause us to exceed our Twitter API rate and connection limits. To make it a singleton, open the config/torquebox.rb file again, and look for the service directive. We need to add a block to this definition that contains the singleton attribute. The configuration should look like this:

TorqueBox/cluster/config/torquebox.rb
```
service TwitterStreamService do
  singleton true
end
```

Now we can deploy with the torquebox deploy command again, and the service will be running on only one node. We can verify this by browsing to the BackStage console for each node at http://<ip-address>:8080/backstage and http://<ip-address>:8180/backstage. Only one instance will have the service running, and it will fail over like our scheduled job did when the master node is stopped.

High-availability singletons are just one example of how TorqueBox cluster nodes can communicate with each other. In this case, the purpose is to coordinate two background jobs so that they are not duplicate. But there are cases where we want to use this communication link for the purpose of duplication, such as when we want to store state on the server. That's when we need to use session replication.

8.5 Using Session Replication

Having a cluster means that each of a single user's requests may be processed on a separate node. There is no guarantee that a value stored in memory during one request cycle will be accessible during the next request cycle. This is especially problematic when we need to remember something a user did.

For example, if our application had a shopping cart, we would want to remember what the user had put in it from page request to page request. Many Rails applications work around this problem by putting session data in an instance of ActiveRecord::SessionStore, which persists user sessions to the database. But putting users' sessions in the database is generally not an optimal solution. In addition to being slow, there is an impedance mismatch between the transience of a user's session and the persistence of a database.

That's why TorqueBox provides a clusterable session store that does require a database. Instead, it uses the Infinispan[7] data grid, which offers a noSQL key-value store that can be replicated across the cluster.

Let's use this session store by adding a new feature to Twitalytics. When a user chooses to retweet a public status, we'll put that tweet into a shopping cart of tweets that lives as long as the session. Then the user can view a list of the status updates they have recently retweeted.

The TorqueBox session store has already been enabled for us by the Rails template we ran in Chapter 6, *Creating a TorqueBox Application*, on page 103. It modified the config/initializers/session_store.rb file by adding this statement:

TorqueBox/cluster/config/initializers/session_store.rb
```
Twitalytics::Application.config.session_store :torquebox_store
```

Now we need to modify the app/controllers/customers_controller.rb so that the retweet() action adds the status object to the session. It should look like this:

TorqueBox/cluster/app/controllers/customers_controller.rb
```
def retweet
  status = Status.find(params[:id])
  status.retweet
  session[:retweets] ||= []
  session[:retweets] << status
  redirect_to customers_path
end
```

Now we can add the code that gets them out of the session and displays them to the user. We'll do this in the dashboard.

---

7. http://www.jboss.org/infinispan

Open the app/controllers/dashboard_controller.rb file, and modify the index() action so that it creates a @retweets variable containing the statuses from the session.

TorqueBox/cluster/app/controllers/dashboard_controller.rb
```
def index
  @retweets = session[:retweets] || []
end
```

Now we need to display the retweets. Open the app/views/dashboard/index.html.erb file, and add this code to the end of the file:

TorqueBox/cluster/app/views/dashboard/index.html.erb
```
<p>
  <% if @retweets.any? %>
    Recent Retweets:
    <ul>
      <% @retweets.each do |retweet|  %>
        <li><%= retweet.status_text %></li>
      <% end %>
    </ul>
  <% end %>
</p>
```

This will iterate over the items in the @retweets variable we created earlier and display a list item for each one. If the list is empty, it will display nothing.

Let's test this. Make sure that both TorqueBox nodes are running and the Apache HTTP Server has been started. There shouldn't be any need to redeploy the Twitalytics because Rails will pick up these changes.

Browse through the proxy to http://<ip-address>:8000/customers/index, and click the Retweet link for one of the statuses. Then look in the consoles of the two TorqueBox nodes and find this statement:

```
12:35:53,959 INFO [stdout] ... Retweeting Status{id=21}
```

Kill that server by pressing Ctrl+C . Then return to the same browser and go to http://<ip-address>:8000/dashboard/index. We'll see our retweet displayed at the bottom of the page even though our request is clearly being processed by the other node.

Session replication is just the tip of the iceberg that is TorqueBox caching. We could use this same mechanism to cache data in our analytics engine and have it distributed across the cluster (even though there is no session associated with the background job). This function could greatly improve the performance of a component that performs calculations and needs to keep indexes or partially computed values on hand.

We've done a lot with our cluster, but we are still managing each node independently. Let's take a look at a feature that allows us to manage the entire cluster from a single controller.

8.6 Running in Domain Mode

The cluster we have set up in this chapter is running in stand-alone mode, which means the life cycle and configuration of each node are independent from the other nodes. But TorqueBox can also run in a more robust domain mode, which introduces a centralized domain controller to the cluster.

In domain mode, we can control the nodes in our cluster from a management interface. We can also simplify our deployment script so that it deploys the application only once (to the domain controller) rather than to multiple hosts. The domain controller then distributes the application across the host nodes for us.

While domain mode is far more powerful, it also involves more setup and a deeper understanding of the underlying JBoss architecture. In its simplest form, we can start a cluster of this type with the following command (make sure you kill the other servers before running this):

```
$ JRUBY_HOME=~/.rvm/rubies/jruby-1.6.7 \
`torquebox env torquebox_home`/jboss/bin/domain.sh
```

The default configuration for domain mode starts two TorqueBox servers in addition to the domain controller. We can deploy to this cluster through the TorqueBox command-line interface, which can be started with the following command:

```
$ torquebox cli
[domain@<ip-address>:9999 /]
```

The [domain@<ip-address>:9999 /] prompt lets us know that we've connected to the controller. There are a number of commands that can be used with this prompt, but we're interested in deploy and undeploy. We can deploy our Knob file thusly:

```
[domain@<ip-address>:9999 /] deploy twitalytics.knob --all-server-groups
```

This pushes the archive to all nodes in the cluster. Then we can undeploy it with this command:

```
[domain@<ip-address>:9999 /] undeploy twitalytics.knob
```

Domain mode is the most powerful way to run a TorqueBox cluster. But you'll probably want to get started with stand-alone mode and work your way up.

Getting serious with domain mode requires modification of the XML files underneath the TORQUEBOX_HOME/jboss/domain/configuration directory and a deeper understanding of how this architecture works.

You can also browse the configuration by visiting the domain console on your local server at http://<ip-address>:9990/]].

8.7 Wrapping Up

We've built a cutting-edge cluster that can power the most demanding workloads imaginable, and it's running a Ruby application!

Our cluster nodes are running behind a proxy that balances the distribution of requests between them by collecting load factors. We're caching our users' session information in a distributed data grid. Our jobs and services are coordinating with each other to ensure maximum performance and data integrity. Best of all, we've done this without any additional infrastructure.

Not only has TorqueBox provided a web server for our JRuby deployment, but it's provided a complete application server. This is as good as performance gets for a Ruby application, and it's how Twitalytics will scale to meet the demands of any workload. But in order for it to perform well, we have to keep it running.

In the next chapter, we'll use some new tools and configuration options to ensure the good health of our JRuby deployment. These techniques will apply not only to TorqueBox but to any of the frameworks covered in this book.

CHAPTER 9

Managing a JRuby Deployment

Deploying an application is only the first step in creating a successful production environment. Keeping it running is the real challenge.

To support any JRuby deployment, it's important that we understand the underlying JVM platform and how it can be configured. In this chapter, you'll learn about the most common start-up options that are needed when booting a JRuby application. They'll help improve both the performance and uptime of our deployment.

To understand how these start-up options affect our runtime, we'll need to gain some insight into the running JVM. To do this, we'll use Java's built-in management console, which provides a graphical tool for tracking resource usage over time.

Configuring runtime options and understanding the management console are important steps in deploying Twitalytics to the wild. With these tools, we'll have everything we need to investigate and diagnose problems on our production server.

Let's begin by booting Twitalytics with these new options.

9.1 Configuring the Runtime

When starting up a JVM, we can configure many different options that affect memory, logging, debugging, profiling, and other runtime characteristics. In this section, we'll take a look at the most commonly used of these options and show how they can be defined for each of the frameworks we've used in this book. Despite the differences in how they are defined, the underlying effects of these options will remain the same across frameworks.

Let's begin with an option that is essential to how JRuby interprets our code.

Setting the Compatibility Version

Every JRuby installation includes both a 1.8 and 1.9 Ruby interpreter. This differs from MRI, which couples a single version of the Ruby language to its runtime. Having both interpreters in one package allows us to choose the version our code will execute against each time we run a program. This option is referred to as the *compatibility version.*

We can set the compatibility version by using the --1.8 and --1.9 options on the ruby command, like this:

```
$ ruby --1.9 -S trinidad
```

Or we can set it globally with the JRUBY_OPTS environment variable.

```
$ export JRUBY_OPTS=--1.9
$ trinidad
```

Either of these two methods is acceptable for running Trinidad or a command-line JRuby application. But TorqueBox allows us to define this value in our config/torquebox.rb with the ruby directive.

```
TorqueBox.configure do
  ruby do
    version "1.9"
  end
end
```

For Warbler, the version can be defined in the config/warbler.rb file with the following statement:

```
config.webxml.jruby.compat.version = "1.9"
```

The effect of setting the version is the same whether we run on Warbler, Trinidad, or TorqueBox. When running in 1.9 mode, we have access to all the latest standard libraries and syntax features. In 1.8 mode, we'll be restricted to the 1.8 standard libraries and syntax.

The default compatibility mode for JRuby 1.6 is version 1.8, but this will be changing to version 1.9 with JRuby 1.7 (see if you can keep that straight).

Let's move on to an option that doesn't have such an obvious impact on how our code is run but is just as important.

Setting the Heap Size

When a JVM starts up, it reserves a chunk of system memory called the *heap.* Each time a new object is created in a JRuby program, the platform allocates a piece of heap memory for it, which is reserved until the garbage collector decides to reclaim the object. At that time, the associated piece of memory is returned to the heap. This process is called *dynamic memory allocation*, and MRI uses a similar strategy. But the JVM gives us more control over how memory is managed.

When we start a JVM, we can configure several parameters that determine how heap memory grows. We can set its initial size, maximum size, and what algorithm the runtime uses for garbage collection. The values we use for these options can greatly affect the performance of our applications. Manually configuring the garbage collection algorithm is an esoteric and rarely needed process because the default JVM collector is almost always sufficient. But it's very common to use the command-line options for setting the heap's size, which are very straightforward.

-J-Xms

> This sets the initial size of the heap. The JVM will reserve this amount of memory at start-up. The flag should be followed by a positive integer value followed by either k, m, or g (for KB, MB, and GB, respectively). Here's an example: -J-Xms64m.

-J-Xmx

> This sets the maximum size of the heap. It should be followed by a positive integer value followed by either k, m, or g (for KB, MB, and GB, respectively). Here's an example: -J-Xmx512m.

The default maximum heap size is 256MB, but most web servers typically run with at least a 512MB cap. If the maximum is set too low, it can cause the JVM to crash. We can demonstrate this by starting up Twitalytics with a ridiculously low maximum of 16MB. Using Trinidad, the command would look like this:

```
$ ruby -J-Xmx16m -S trinidad
...
Error: Your application used more memory than the safety cap of 16m.
Specify -J-Xmx####m to increase it (#### = cap size in MB).
Specify -w for full OutOfMemoryError stack trace
```

With reasonable memory settings, we might run into this error if Twitalytics started leaking memory. But with a stable application, it is not something we should ordinarily see.

The memory options we'll use with TorqueBox are similar to the command shown previously, but we pass them to the torquebox command as a single string. A reasonable configuration might look like this:

```
$ torquebox run -J="\-Xmx1024m \-Xms256m"
```

Using these options with Warbler and the java command is also different because we no longer need the -J prefix, which is specific to JRuby. It would look like this:

```
$ java -Xmx1024m -Xms256m -jar twitalytics.war
```

The JVM's cap on memory consumption may seem like a frustrating antifeature, but it protects against the JVM reserving every last bit of system memory at runtime. Having a JVM crash is much more pleasant than having an entire system crash. Once we know the amount of memory an application needs, the cap becomes a safety net instead of a road block.

Determining the best maximum and minimum sizes for the heap is an iterative process. After running Twitalytics in a staging environment, we'll learn where its memory consumption tops out, and we can set the our boundaries accordingly. The JVM provides some excellent tools that can help us with this by displaying memory consumption over time. We'll discuss these in Section 9.2, *Inspecting the Runtime with JMX*, on page 167. But first, we have one more command option to add.

Setting the Execution Mode

Most JVM implementations can run in two execution modes, which are configured at start-up time by setting either the --client or --server flag to enable client and server execution modes, respectively. Each mode determines, among other things, how the JVM will optimize bytecode at execution. Each mode is described next:

--client

In client mode, a program's start-up time and memory usage are minimized. This is particularly good in the case of a local desktop application where you usually want to start it up fast and it won't be left running for days on end. Client mode is also the default execution mode on most 32-bit JVMs.

--server

In server mode, the JVM optimizes itself for runtime speed. This results in a slightly slower start-up time and higher memory consumption. The advantage is that the JVM will dynamically optimize bytecode during execution. For example, it will optimize inner loops. Thus, an application will become faster after running for while—after it has warmed up. This process is called *just-in-time* (JIT) compilation.

In almost all cases where we are running a web application, we'll want to use the --server mode. We can start Twitalytics and any other JRuby application in this mode by passing the option directly to the ruby or java command. For Trinidad, the command is this:

```
$ ruby --server -S trinidad
```

With TorqueBox, the command is this:

```
$ torquebox run -J="\-server"
```

But for the executable WAR file we created with Warbler, the command is this (note that there is one less hyphen when passing the option directly to the java command):

```
$ java -server -jar twitalytics.war
```

It's also important to note that the JRE does not include a server mode. This is one of the reasons it's usually beneficial to install the JDK on a production server.

All of the options we've discussed in this section can improve the health of a JRuby application. But we still need a way to keep an eye on how the runtime is doing. That's why the JVM provides built-in management extensions.

9.2 Inspecting the Runtime with JMX

Java Management Extensions (JMX) is a set of tools that support the management and monitoring of system objects, devices, networking, and applications. All of these tools are exposed through a service interface that can be controlled by scripts and even other applications. But the JDK comes packaged with a general-purpose console that provides a graphical interface for quickly inspecting a runtime through these extensions.

Before we start the JMX console, let's boot our application. When doing so, we'll provide the --manage option, which turns on JRuby's own management extensions. Using Trinidad, the command is this:

```
$ ruby --manage -S trinidad
```

But when running from a WAR file created by Warbler, there is no option to pass because we are invoking Java directly. Instead, we need to add two options to the java command, which are the same options the --manage flag adds behind the scenes.

```
$ java -Dcom.sun.management.jmxremote -Djruby.management.enabled=true \
     -jar twitalytics.war
```

With TorqueBox, this option isn't necessary because the JMX services are exposed by default.

No matter which framework we choose to run Twitalytics on, we can open the management console with the following command:

```
$ jconsole
```

This command is provided by the JDK we installed in *Preface*, on page xi. When the JConsole starts up, it will give us the choice of connecting to a local JVM or a remote JVM. In the list of local JVMs, we'll see the process we started earlier. This is shown in Figure 29, *The JConsole start-up screen*, on page 169. When we select this process, JConsole will connect to the JVM.

The JConsole Overview page, which is pictured in Figure 30, *The JConsole Overview page*, on page 170, provides near-real-time graphical views of heap usage, CPU usage, active threads, and the number of classes loaded in the runtime. These views are useful when trying to track down memory leaks, misbehaving threads, and many other problems. There is a vast amount of information in this console—so much so that entire books are written about it. But it's not necessary to be an expert from the start.

Let's take a look at the Memory screen, which is pictured in Figure 31, *The JConsole Memory page*, on page 171. While the Overview screen showed us only heap usage, the Memory screen gives us complete insight into the different categories of JVM memory usage. There is even a button that allows us to invoke the garbage collector directly. Go ahead and click it. You'll see a dip in the memory usage graph shortly after you do. The garbage collector reclaimed all the objects on the heap that were not referenced by the application. This released the memory associated with those objects, which caused the graph of heap usage to dip.

Let's move on to the MBean screen. An MBean, or managed bean, is an object that represents a resource in the JVM that can be managed. Each MBean will have attributes that tell us about the resource and the operations we can invoke on it.

If we explore the directorylike structure in the left panel of the screen, we'll find MBeans that represent the different components of Tomcat and the JRuby runtime. Let's browse to the Tomcat/ThreadPool/http-bio-3000 bean, which represents the thread pool that is listening for HTTP requests on port 3000 of our localhost. Even though the MBean's name gives this information away, we can make certain of this by selecting the Attributes node under it. The port attribute defines the port number, and the running attribute tells us that it is working.

Figure 29—The JConsole start-up screen

Next, let's select the Operations node. We'll see buttons that represent the management operations we can execute against this MBean, as pictured in Figure 32, *The JConsole MBean page*, on page 172. Click the unbind() button, which fittingly unbinds this thread pool from its port. Now when we point a browser to http://localhost:3000, we won't see Twitalytics. We'll also find that the value of the running attribute of the MBean has changed to false.

We can rebind the thread pool to the port if we invoke the bind() operation and then the start() operation by clicking their respective buttons. We'll find that the value of the running attribute of the MBean has returned to true, and Twitalytics is available again at http://localhost:3000.

JMX provides an excellent mechanism for managing our application, but clicking buttons in a GUI may not be your preferred tool. In the next section, we'll invoke an MBean programmatically.

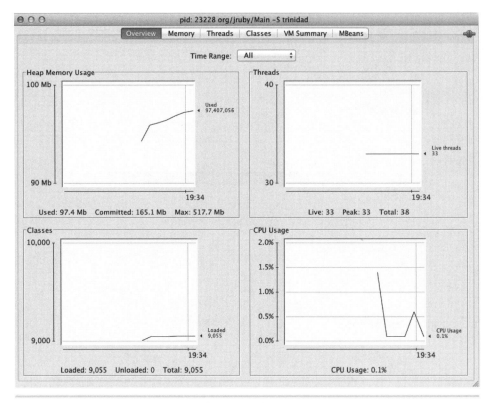

Figure 30—The JConsole Overview page

9.3 Managing the Runtime with JMX

JConsole is just one way to use the JMX services that are exposed by the JVM. We can also build our own clients that consume JMX services. This is a handy way to write tools that we can use to manage our applications.

To create a JMX client, we'll need to use some tools that can speak to the JMX interfaces. Fortunately, the jmx4r gem provides a Ruby wrapper for this Java-based protocol.

Let's install the jmx4r gem with the following command:

```
$ gem install jmx4r
```

Before using this gem, we'll need to make sure a JRuby server is running. Let's use Trinidad again.

```
$ ruby --manage -S trinidad
```

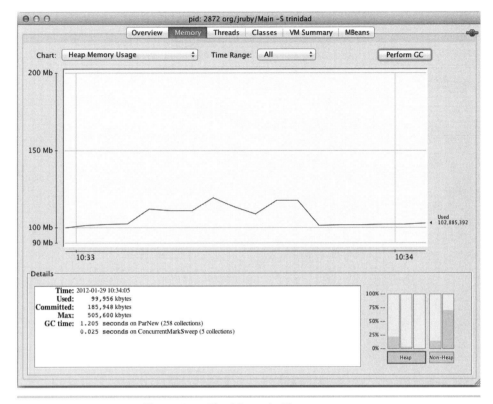

Figure 31—The JConsole Memory page

Now we can connect to the JMX services in the Trinidad process from the shell. We'll begin by starting an IRB session and requiring the jmx4r gem.

```
$ irb
jruby-1.6.7 :001 > require 'rubygems'
=> true
jruby-1.6.7 :002 > require 'jmx4r'
=> true
```

Next, we'll create a connection to the Trinidad process with the following command:

```
jruby-1.6.7 :004 > JMX::MBean.establish_connection \
                   :command => "org/jruby/Main -S trinidad"
 => #<JMX::MBeanServerConnectionProxy:0x7e64cfe0 @connection=#<#<Class:0x5...
```

The :command argument matches the connection string we saw in the initial JConsole dialog. But the gem also supports connecting to remote JVM processes with the :host, :port, :username, and :password arguments.

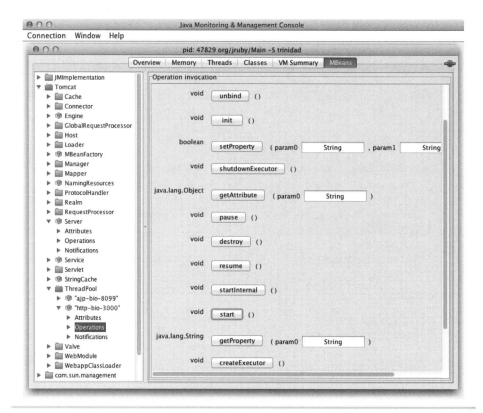

Figure 32—The JConsole MBean page

Now that we've created a connection, we can get a handle to one of the MBeans. We'll use the Memory manager:

```
jruby-1.6.7 :005 > memory = JMX::MBean.find_by_name "java.lang:type=Memory"
 => #<JMX::MBean:0x1916a3de>
```

Now we can invoke some operations on the MBean. We'll use the gc() method, which performs the same action as when we click the Perform GC button in the JConsole. Execute this statement:

```
jruby-1.6.7 :007 > memory.gc
 => nil
```

If the JConsole is still open, we'll see another dip in the graph of heap memory usage. Running the garbage collector is a nice example, but it's not something we'll usually need in the JVM. It's possible that we might want to unbind and rebind our HTTP connector, as we did in the previous section. But a more useful example would invoke our own custom MBean. Let's create one and invoke it from a Rake task.

9.4 Creating a Management Bean

The purpose of an MBean is to help manage our application. Many Ruby applications provide this same kind of interface with RESTful services, but those tend to get in the way of the real application. MBeans provide a better interface because they are separated from the rest of the application, which means they have their own security, port, and graphical interface. As a result, there is less of a chance that an ordinary user will accidentally (or intentionally) gain access to the management services.

Let's create an MBean that we can use to manage the logging level of our Rails application. We'll start by adding the jmx4r gem to our Gemfile and running Bundler.

Management/twitalytics/Gemfile
```
gem 'jmx4r'
```

Next, we'll create a lib/logging_bean.rb file and add the following code to it:

Management/twitalytics/lib/logging_bean.rb
```
class LoggingBean < JMX::DynamicMBean
  operation "Set the Rails log level"
  parameter :int, "level", "the new log level"
  returns :string
  def set_log_level(level)
    Rails.logger.level = level
    "Set log level to #{Rails.logger.level}"
  end
end
```

This class inherits from the JMX::DynamicMBean class, which hides all of the Java code that goes into creating an MBean. Then it defines a set_log_level(level) operation and declares its argument type and return value type. Unlike Ruby, Java is a strongly typed language, so it expects these things. In the body of the set_log_level(level) operation, we're setting Rails.logger.level to the value that was passed in as an argument.

Next, we need to register this MBean with the platform's MBean server, which is part of the JVM runtime. We'll do this by creating an mbeans.rb initializer file in the config/initializers directory and putting the following code in it:

Management/twitalytics/config/initializers/mbeans.rb
```
java_import "javax.management.ObjectName"
java_import "java.lang.management.ManagementFactory"
```

This is the closest we'll come to writing Java code in this book. We've imported two Java classes that will give us access to the MBean server.

Next, we'll add the code that instantiates our bean and registers it with the server. Put these lines of code after the java_import statements:

Management/twitalytics/config/initializers/mbeans.rb
```
mbean = LoggingBean.new
object_name = ObjectName.new("twitalytics:name=LoggingBean")

mbean_server = ManagementFactory.platform_mbean_server
mbean_server.register_mbean mbean, object_name
```

Let's run Trinidad again and look for our MBean in the JConsole (reboot the server if it's already running).

```
$ ruby --manage -S trinidad
```

Run jconsole and navigate to the MBeans screen. We'll see a twitlaytics MBean with the operation we defined. When we enter a value in the text field of the set_log_level(level) method and click the button, we'll see a result as pictured in Figure 33, *Invoking a custom MBean*, on page 175.

Now let's write a Rake task that invokes this MBean service for us. Create a lib/tasks/mbean.rake file, and add the following code to it:

Management/twitalytics/lib/tasks/mbean.rake
```
namespace :log do
  task :debug do
    JMX::MBean.establish_connection :command => "org/jruby/Main -S trinidad"
    logging = JMX::MBean.find_by_name "twitalytics:name=LoggingBean"
    puts logging.set_log_level(0)
  end
end
```

The steps in this task are similar to the steps we executed in our IRB session earlier in the chapter. But instead of getting a handle to the Memory MBean, we're retrieving our custom MBean.

Let's try our new task. If the server is still running, we can execute this command:

```
$ rake log:debug
Set log level to 0
```

That should feel a little more natural to a Rubyist than using the GUI. But the graphical choice is always there, and it can be useful when someone other than you is managing your application (such as an operations team).

Let's move on and use some other tools to get even more insight into our running application.

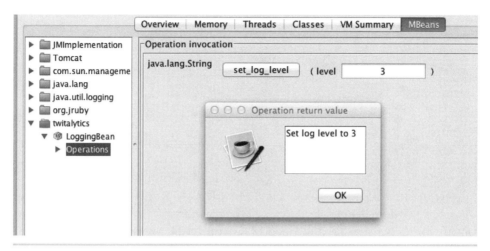

Figure 33—Invoking a custom MBean

9.5 Profiling an Application

Most of the third-party profiling and performance management tools that we use with MRI-based deployments will also work with JRuby. But in addition to these external tools, JRuby provides an internal profiler that can be used to inspect the runtime characteristics of our applications. We'll look at both kinds of profilers in this section, but we'll start with one of the most powerful third-party tools.

Using the New Relic Gem

New Relic[1] is a popular Ruby profiling tool that is compatible with JRuby. It works by running an agent on a host server that reports information back to the New Relic servers. We can then log into the New Relic dashboard to view an analysis of the data that was collected.

To use New Relic with Twitalytics, we need to create a New Relic account[2] and include the newrelic_rpm gem in our Gemfile.

```
gem "newrelic_rpm"
```

Then, we'll create a config/newrelic.yml configuration file, which contains the license key and configuration for how the New Relic agent will monitor each environment. It should look something like this:

---

1. http://newrelic.com/
2. http://newrelic.com/signup

Management/twitalytics/config/newrelic.yml

```
common: &default_settings
  license_key: '******************************'
  app_name: Twitalytics
staging:
  <<: *default_settings
  monitor_mode: true
production:
  <<: *default_settings
  monitor_mode: false
```

Once the application is deployed, the agent will begin to report back to the New Relic server. The dashboard will provide us with insight and analysis of trends in the data. This will help us diagnosis memory leaks, pages that load slowly, database queries that need to be optimized, and many other things.

New Relic is a powerful, production-grade tool. But in development, it may be helpful to use something simpler.

Using the JRuby Profiler

Let's play around with JRuby's built-in profiler. Move to the ~/code/twitalytics directory, and check out the trinidad branch. Then run the following command:

```
$ ruby --profile -S trinidad
```

Make a few page requests, and then kill the process by pressing Ctrl+C. This will dump some statistics to the console that look like this:

```
main thread profile results:
Total time: 57.00

      total      self    children      calls  method
      -------------------------------------------------------------
      53.50      0.00      53.50          2  Kernel#load
      48.49      0.00      48.49          1  Trinidad::Server#start
      26.83     26.83       0.00          1  Java::OrgApacheCatalinaCore:...
      21.65     21.65       0.00          1  Java::OrgApacheCatalinaStart...
       5.38      0.10       5.28        716  Kernel#require
       4.99      0.00       4.99       7499  Class#new
       4.52      0.00       4.52        320  Kernel#require
       4.08      0.31       3.77      30174  Array#each
       3.74      0.00       3.74          1  Trinidad::Server#initialize
       3.72      0.00       3.72          1  Trinidad::Server#load_tomcat_...
       3.58      0.00       3.58         11  Hash#each
       3.56      0.00       3.56          1  Trinidad::Extensions.configur...
       3.56      0.01       3.55        856  Gem::Specification.each
       3.27      0.00       3.27          8  Trinidad::Extensions.extension
       3.27      0.00       3.27          6  Trinidad::Extensions.load_ext...
  ...
```

We can tell from this dump that the main program loop is controlled by the Trinidad::Server#start() method. We can also see from the line corresponding to the Trinidad::Extensions.load_extension() method that loading our extensions takes about three seconds. This kind of information can be useful when things get stuck. But using the profiler with a complete application usually leaves us swimming in irrelevant data. In some cases, this may be what you want, but it's usually better to isolate the code we want to profile. For example, we can profile just the standard_dev(values) method from the Twitalytics AnalyticsUtil module because it processes a big array like this:

```
$ ruby -r lib/analytics_util.rb --profile \
-e "AnalyticsUtil.standard_dev(Array.new(10**4) {1})"
Profiling enabled; ^C shutdown will now dump profile info

main thread profile results:
Total time: 0.46

        total     self    children      calls  method
-----------------------------------------------------------------
        0.44      0.00      0.44          15  Kernel#require
        0.12      0.11      0.01          12  JavaUtilities#get_proxy_or_p...
        0.11      0.00      0.11           5  Java::Java.method_missing
        0.09      0.01      0.08          53  Object.method_added
        0.08      0.00      0.08         111  Object.method_added
...
```

That still generates a lot of information, but it's a little more tractable. Let's break things down even more. The built-in profiler also includes a graph mode, which separates the execution times of callers and callees. We can demonstrate this by running the previous example with the --profile.graph option:

```
$ ruby -r lib/analytics_util.rb --profile.graph \
-e "AnalyticsUtil.standard_dev(Array.new(10**4) {1})"
Profiling enabled; ^C shutdown will now dump profile info

Total time: 0.55

%total  %self    total     self    children    calls  name
-----------------------------------------------------------------------
                  0.60      0.00      0.60       1/1   JRuby::Profiler.profile
108%     0%       0.60      0.00      0.60         1   JRuby::Profiler.prof...
                  0.36      0.00      0.36       2/2   Enumerable#inject
                  0.25      0.17      0.08       1/1   Array#collect
                  0.00      0.00      0.00       1/1   Math#sqrt
                  0.00      0.00      0.00       2/4   Array#length
                  0.00      0.00      0.00       2/2   Fixnum#/
                  0.00      0.00      0.00      1/20   Array#empty?
...
```

Graph mode gives us a better picture of why certain methods are taking up time and which callers are contributing the most to that time. But it displays a list of every method that gets called, which means we are still pretty inundated with information. Let's keep breaking things down.

The JRuby profiler also includes an API that we can use to instrument our code and narrow down the part of our application that gets profiled. Let's try this in our AnalyticsUtil. Open the lib/analytics_util.rb file and modify the standard_dev() method so it looks like this:

```
def self.standard_dev(vals)
  profile_data = JRuby::Profiler.profile do
    if vals.empty?
      0
    else
      avg = (vals.inject(0) {|sum, s| sum + s}) / vals.size
      diffs = vals.map {|s| (s-avg)**2}
      Math.sqrt((diffs.inject(0) {|sum, s| sum + s}) / vals.size)
    end
  end
  profile_printer = JRuby::Profiler::GraphProfilePrinter.new(profile_data)
  profile_printer.printProfile(STDOUT)
end
```

We're wrapping the body of the standard_dev() method in a block that gets passed to the JRuby::Profiler.profile() method. This returns some profiler data, which we pass to the JRuby::Profiler::GraphProfilePrinter class so it can be printed in graph mode.

Now let's run our example with the --profile.api option, which will turn on the API mode. We'll also need to require the jruby/profiler package, which contains the classes we added to the AnalyticsUtil. The command will look like the code shown in Figure 34, *Example command with --profile.api*, on page 179.

Now we've isolated our profiling down to just the code that's relevant, and we're getting a more concise picture of the performance metrics for our standard deviation method.

With TorqueBox, we can enable the profiling API by setting the profile_api directive to true in our config/torquebox.rb file like this:

```
TorqueBox.configure do
  profile_api true
end
```

Both the New Relic gem and the JRuby profiler are tools that can help us solve problems as well as prevent them, but they aren't the only options. Because Twitalytics is running on JRuby, we have access to a massive collection of performance analysis tools. As with our deployment tools, using JRuby

```
$ ruby -r lib/analytics_util.rb -r jruby/profiler --profile.api \
-e "AnalyticsUtil.standard_dev(Array.new(10**4) {1})"
Profiling enabled; ^C shutdown will now dump profile info

Total time: 0.68

%total   %self    total    self   children      calls  name
-----------------------------------------------------------------------
  100%     0%      0.68    0.00     0.68            1  (top)
                   0.40    0.00     0.40          2/2  Enumerable#inject
                   0.28    0.18     0.11          1/1  Array#collect
                   0.00    0.00     0.00          1/1  Math#sqrt
                   0.00    0.00     0.00          2/4  Array#length
                   0.00    0.00     0.00          2/2  Fixnum#/
                   0.00    0.00     0.00          1/1  Array#empty?
-----------------------------------------------------------------------
                   0.40    0.00     0.40          2/2  (top)
   58%     0%      0.40    0.00     0.40            2  Enumerable#inject
                   0.40    0.40     0.00          2/2  Array#each
-----------------------------------------------------------------------
                   0.40    0.40     0.00          2/2  Enumerable#inject
   58%    58%      0.40    0.40     0.00            2  Array#each
-----------------------------------------------------------------------
                   0.28    0.18     0.11          1/1  (top)
   41%    25%      0.28    0.18     0.11            1  Array#collect
                   0.11    0.11     0.00    10000/10000  Fixnum#**
-----------------------------------------------------------------------
                   0.11    0.11     0.00    10000/10000  Array#collect
   15%    15%      0.11    0.11     0.00        10000  Fixnum#**
```

Figure 34—Example command with –profile.api

doesn't mean we have to dramatically change the way we do things. But if we are willing to embrace some new tools, we'll gain a lot of power.

9.6 Wrapping Up

Keeping an application running is difficult. But the tools and techniques we've used in this chapter will help us diagnose and resolve problems when our application starts misbehaving. In this chapter, you've learned about the essential configuration options required to run a JRuby application in production. There are many other options we did not discuss, and they are worth exploring. But the ones we've covered will get you well on your way to a successful production JRuby deployment.

You've also learned about the Java Management Extensions, which helped us inspect and control our production runtime. You may choose not to use this tool, but it still helped us gain a better understanding of the JVM's innards.

Finally, we used some profiling tools to get a snapshot of Twitalytics' performance characteristics. Every application has its slow spots, but with a basic understanding of these tools, you'll be able to track down those pain points without much trouble.

Deploying Twitalytics on JRuby has simplified our infrastructure, which enables these tools to give us a better picture of the health of our system. We no longer have to monitor dozens of processes that have their own memory footprints and CPU utilization. Instead, we can use the robust tools and services provided by the JVM to capture the entire picture of our application's performance.

In the next chapter, we'll move away from our production runtime and take a look at the bigger picture of how we get our code out to customers. We'll explore a deployment technique that's been alluded to in some of the earlier chapters.

CHAPTER 10

Using a Continuous Integration Server

Continuous integration (CI) is the process of applying quality control validations to a code base every time it changes. In the case of Twitalytics and most Ruby applications, this means running RSpec after each commit. But it's not enough to rely on developers to run these tests because their local environments may differ from our production environment. Developers do lots of stuff on their computers that can affect a test run (such as installing software and setting environment variables). To ensure the reliability of our tests, we need to run them the same way every time. This principle also applies to our deployments.

When we deploy from our development machines to production, we run the risk of our local configuration affecting the artifacts we published. But a CI server can provide a static environment that resembles the production server. The result will be a more consistent and reliable process for publishing releases of our software.

At the very least, we should be deploying Twitalytics to a staging server before we send it on to production. This would give us an opportunity to validate any changes we've made to the application and our deployment process before going live. But even with a staging server, we should not deploy directly from our development machines. We need to deploy from an environment that won't be affected by local configuration changes. This is the role a continuous integration server plays.

In this chapter, we'll introduce continuous integration into our process by using the Jenkins CI server[1] to run our tests and deploy Twitalytics to a staging server. This will give us not only continuous integration but also continuous deployment. Let's begin by getting to know Jenkins.

---

1. http://jenkins-ci.org/

10.1 Installing Jenkins

Jenkins is an open source application for continuously building and testing software. An excellent publicly available example of a running Jenkins instance is the TorqueBox CI service,[2] which is hosted by the same CloudBees platform we set up for Warbler in Chapter 3, *Deploying an Archive File*, on page 37.

We'll use Jenkins to test our application and deploy it each time changes are pushed to our repository. But rather than setting up a cloud-based or virtual CI server, we'll run Jenkins on our development machine. There are several binary distributions of Jenkins for specific platforms, but we'll use the executable WAR file distribution. It is similar to the executable WAR file we created for Twitalytics in Chapter 1, *Getting Started with JRuby*, on page 1. This will ensure that the steps in the chapter are the same on all platforms.

We'll start by downloading the WAR file from the official Jenkins website.[3] Put the downloaded file into your home directory and run it with the following command (but make sure you don't already have Warbler or TorqueBox running because they use the same ports):

```
$ java -jar jenkins.war
```

Our Jenkins server is running. We can browse to http://localhost:8080, and we'll see the Jenkins dashboard, as pictured in Figure 35, *The Jenkins dashboard*, on page 183. There is a Manage Jenkins link in the left navigation pane of that page. Follow it and then click the Manage Plugins link on the next page. On the plug-ins page, select the Available tab. This will bring up a list of plug-ins that we can install to our Jenkins server.

Look for the Jenkins GIT plug-in and check the box next to it. Then click the "Install without restart" button at the bottom of the page. When the installation completes, return to the Jenkins dashboard at http://localhost:8080.

Our CI server is ready do some work. But before we can add a job that runs our tests, we'll need to tell Jenkins how to access our code. To do this, we'll create a depot for our Git repository.

10.2 Creating a Git Depot

A Git depot is a bare clone of a Git repository, which means it's a repository that does not have a staging area where edits can be made and committed.

Figure 35—The Jenkins dashboard

Instead, it can only be pushed to and pulled from. A depot is usually used to share changes between distributed copies of the repository. The best example of this is a GitHub project.

We need to create a depot for our Twitalytics repository so that Jenkins can check out our code and run the tests against it. We could do this by pushing our code to GitHub or a similar service, but we'll use a local depot for this example.

We need to clone our Twitalytics repository with the --bare option to create our depot. We'll direct it to the ~/depot/twitalytics.git directory like this:

```
$ git clone --bare ~/code/twitalytics ~/depot/twitalytics.git
```

Next, we'll add the clone as the remote origin in our Twitalytics repository.

```
$ cd ~/code/twitalytics
$ git remote add origin ~/depot/twitalytics.git/
```

This allows us to push to the depot thusly:

```
$ git push depot
Everything up-to-date
```

Everything is already up-to-date because we haven't made any changes since we cloned the repository.

Our Git depot is ready. Now we'll set up Jenkins to use it.

10.3 Creating a Jenkins Job

Jenkins uses the concept of a job to represent any kind of user-defined task. A job can run our tests, migrate a database, push a WAR file out to a server, or run static analysis tools like Brakeman[4] that provide reports on code correctness. A job can even do things that are unrelated to our application, such as installing software packages on the host. The possibilities are basically endless.

We're going to create a job that runs the steps we used to deploy Twitalytics in Chapter 3, *Deploying an Archive File*, on page 37. This will automate our build process and make it more consistent. Let's browse to the Jenkins dashboard at http://localhost:8080 and follow the Create New Jobs link on the front page. This will bring us to the page pictured in Figure 36, *Creating a Jenkins job*, on page 185. We need to enter *twitalytics* for the name of the job, select "Build a free-style software project," and then click the OK button (as shown in the figure).

This takes us to a page containing a form we can use to configure our job. Scroll down to the Source Code Management section and fill in the Git repository with the location of our Twitalytics depot, as pictured in Figure 37, *Connecting Jenkins to a Git repository*, on page 185 (note that you'll need to replace the ~ with the full path to your depot). We also fill in the branch specifier with warbler because that's the version of Twitalytics we are going to build and deploy. Each time this job runs, it will check out a fresh copy of our *warbler* branch to ensure that it's testing and deploying the latest code.

Next, we need to scroll down to the Build section. Select the "Add build step" drop-down and choose "Execute shell" or "Execute Windows batch command" depending on your platform. This will reveal a Command textbox that we need to fill in with the steps for running our tests and deployment, like this:

```
bundle install
RAILS_ENV=test bundle exec rake db:drop
RAILS_ENV=test bundle exec rake db:setup
RAILS_ENV=test bundle exec rspec spec/
bundle exec rake deploy:war
```

These commands will install our dependencies, create a fresh database, and run our tests. If the tests succeed, Jenkins will run the deploy:war task we created in Chapter 3, *Deploying an Archive File*, on page 37, which creates a new WAR file and pushes it out to our virtual server.

---

4. http://brakemanscanner.org/

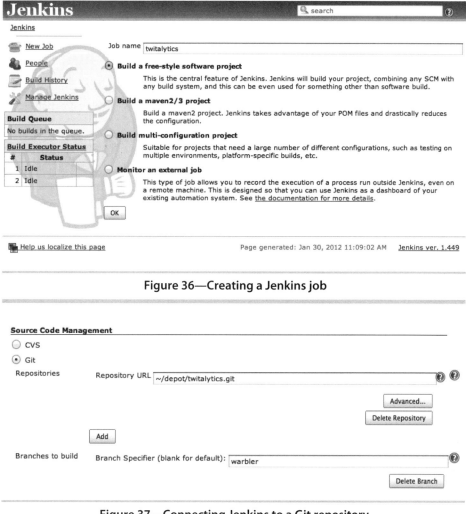

Figure 36—Creating a Jenkins job

Figure 37—Connecting Jenkins to a Git repository

Next, we need to scroll to the bottom of the page and click the Save button. Our job is ready to be run, but we first need to ensure that our deployment target is running. Let's move to the Twitalytics repository, check out the Warbler branch, and start Vagrant like this:

```
$ cd ~/code/twitalytics
$ git checkout warbler
$ vagrant up
```

Now we can execute our Jenkins job. We'll do this manually for now and automate it later. Browse to the Jenkins dashboard, and click the "twitalytics" link for our job. Then click the Build Now link on the page that follows. Shortly after clicking this, we'll see the job show up in the build queue on the bottom left of the page.

When the job finishes, the gray dot next to its entry in the queue will turn blue. This means the job was successful. We can check this out by pointing a browser to http://localhost:8888, where we'll see Twitalytics running on the virtual machine.

Let's take a closer look at what happened. Click the entry for the most recent build in the queue on the "twitalytics" job page. Then, we'll follow the Console Output link, which will take us to a page with the full output of job, as pictured below (if the production database has already been migrated, we won't see the schema changes):

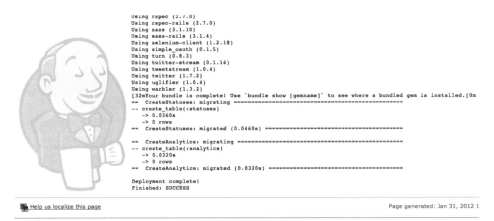

```
Using rspec (2.7.0)
Using rspec-rails (2.7.0)
Using sass (3.1.10)
Using sass-rails (3.1.4)
Using selenium-client (1.2.18)
Using simple_oauth (0.1.5)
Using turn (0.8.3)
Using twitter-stream (0.1.14)
Using tweetstream (1.0.4)
Using twitter (1.7.2)
Using uglifier (1.0.4)
Using warbler (1.3.2)
[32mYour bundle is complete! Use `bundle show [gemname]` to see where a bundled gem is installed.[0m
== CreateStatuses: migrating ===========================================
-- create_table(:statuses)
   -> 0.0360s
   -> 0 rows
== CreateStatuses: migrated (0.0460s) ==================================

== CreateAnalytics: migrating ==========================================
-- create_table(:analytics)
   -> 0.0320s
   -> 0 rows
== CreateAnalytics: migrated (0.0320s) =================================

Deployment complete!
Finished: SUCCESS
```

Help us localize this page   Page generated: Jan 31, 2012 1

Our CI job is working! Now we'll set it up to run automatically so we don't have click the Build Now link every time we want it to run. On the Configuration page for the job, scroll down to the Build Triggers section, and select the Poll SCM box. In the text field below it, enter the cron string * * * * *, as pictured in Figure 38, *Configuring Jenkins to poll the SCM repository for changes*, on page 187. This will schedule the server to poll the Git depot for changes every minute. If it finds that new changes have been checked in since the last build, it will run the job again. Click the Save button to make sure our change is remembered.

Before we wrap things up, let's make sure we save the WAR file artifact that is generated for each successful execution of the job.

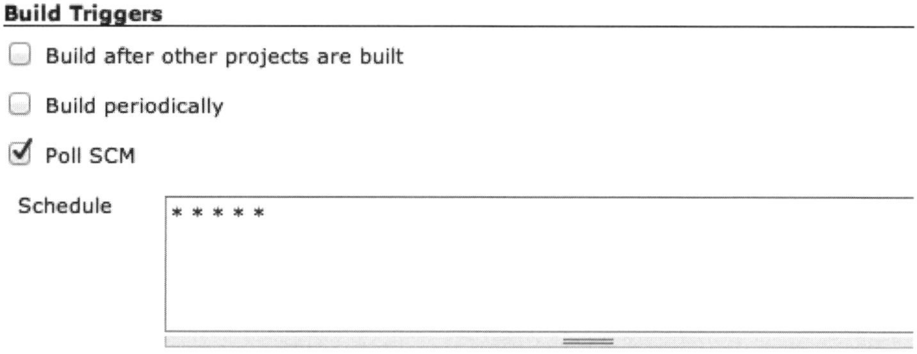

Build Triggers

☐ Build after other projects are built

☐ Build periodically

☑ Poll SCM

Schedule

```
* * * * *
```

Figure 38—Configuring Jenkins to poll the SCM repository for changes

10.4 Archiving Artifacts with Jenkins

One of the advantages of using an archive file for deployment is that we can use it to easily store, validate, and redeploy versions of our application. That's why Jenkins allows us to archive the artifacts that are generated from a successful build. Let's configure our CI job to make use of this.

Browse to the configuration page for the Twitalytics job, and scroll down to the bottom. Under the section Post-build Actions, select the Archive Artifacts box. In the textbox below it, enter *twitalytics.war*, as pictured in Figure 39, *Archiving artifacts generated by a successful build*, on page 188. Click the Save button, and return to the job page.

Next, we need to click the Build Now link to force the job to run again (since no changes have been made to our repository). After the job has completed, a new artifact will be created under the ~/.jenkins/jobs/twitalytics/lastSuccessful/ directory. We can see it like this:

```
$ ls ~/.jenkins/jobs/twitalytics/lastSuccessful/archive/
twitalytics.war
```

The lastSuccessful directory is actually a symlink to a directory named for a particular build number. When new builds run, we'll still be able to access our old artifacts like this:

```
$ ls ~/.jenkins/jobs/twitalytics/builds/2/archive/
twitalytics.war
```

Now that we have this artifact stored on our CI server, we can use it to do a number of things. We have the ability to create Jenkins jobs that use it. We can create jobs that deploy it to different environments, and we can have a

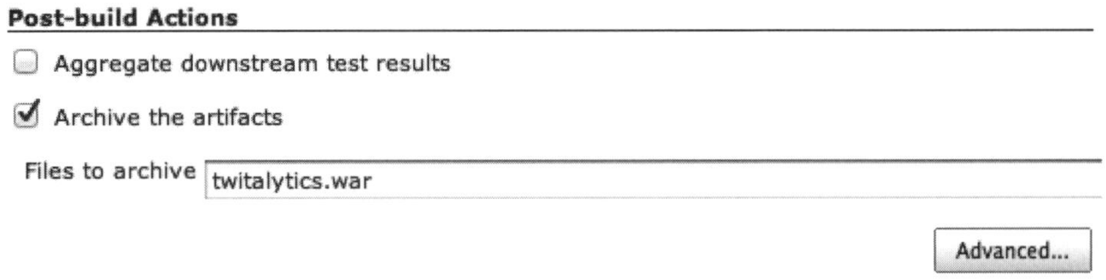

Post-build Actions

☐ Aggregate downstream test results

☑ Archive the artifacts

Files to archive | twitalytics.war

Advanced...

Figure 39—Archiving artifacts generated by a successful build

job validate its MD5 hash to make sure it hasn't been tampered with or corrupted. We can also roll back to previous successful versions of our application or ship the archive off to an operations team that deploys the artifact for us.

We've used a WAR file in this example, but we could follow the same steps with a TorqueBox Knob file. Unfortunately, Trinidad does not support any kind of standard packaging, so there is no artifact we can archive. But we could still use Jenkins to deploy Trinidad with Capistrano.

There are many different kinds of jobs that can be created in Jenkins. Any task that requires a centralized and consistent environment for execution should be run on a CI server.

10.5 Wrapping Up

We've turned our development environment into a CI server. But setting up Jenkins on a dedicated CI server or cloud-based server would require the same process and configuration. Once we've moved CI into its own environment, we can begin to change the way we manage our infrastructure.

If all deployments are run from the CI server, we no longer need to give developers access to the staging or production server. We can lock them down so that deployments come from only a single source. This can improve the consistency and reliability of our application.

Building and deploying from a CI server is an essential part of an effective deployment process. It ensures that our code is reliable by testing it in an isolated and consistent environment before sending it out to the world.

But adopting continuous integration is more than just using new tools. It can also change the end-to-end process we use to deliver software to our customers. It's the first step on the path to continuous deployment, which can greatly improve a development team's ability to respond to bugs and failures. This can relieve many of our deployment problems but not all.

The most difficult part of deployment is that every environment is different. Technologies, processes, and team expertise all play a role in determining how an application will be delivered to customers. This makes it difficult to reuse and create reusable deployment tools. As a result, the individuals responsible for a deployment have to be intimately familiar with the technologies they are working with.

This book has provided a survey of the frameworks and tools that can be used to support a JRuby deployment. But as you go forth and build more advanced and complex applications, you'll need to dig deeper into the particular technologies you've chosen for your product. There is nothing more helpful to this task than the support of the community.

The communities that surround the JRuby technologies are some of the most helpful and supportive in the industry. The JRuby core team actively addresses issues on the mailing list and on IRC. The TorqueBox and Trinidad teams are equally helpful. The technologies covered in this book are all in their infancy, but the number of users adopting them is growing rapidly. As a result, there are many developers who have worked through some of the problems you'll encounter, and they'll often share their wisdom on the mailing lists.

Likewise, it is important that you share what you learn with the community. As you grow in your ability to run and manage a JRuby application, be sure to help others, because they may one day help you.

Index

Ruby on the JVM and More Languages

Want to integrate Ruby within your Enterprise JVM environment? JRuby is the answer. And when you're ready to expand your horizons, we've got seven major languages worthy of your study.

Now you can bring the best of Ruby into the world of Java, with *Using JRuby*. Come to the source for the JRuby core team's insights and insider tips. You'll learn how to call Java objects seamlessly from Ruby, and deal with Java idioms such as interfaces and overloaded functions. Run Ruby code from Java, and make a Java program scriptable in Ruby. See how to compile Ruby into .class files that are callable from Java, Scala, Clojure, or any other JVM language.

Charles O Nutter, Thomas Enebo, Nick Sieger, Ola Bini, and Ian Dees
(300 pages) ISBN: 9781934356654. $34.95
http://pragprog.com/titles/jruby

You should learn a programming language every year, as recommended by *The Pragmatic Programmer*. But if one per year is good, how about *Seven Languages in Seven Weeks*? In this book you'll get a hands-on tour of Clojure, Haskell, Io, Prolog, Scala, Erlang, and Ruby. Whether or not your favorite language is on that list, you'll broaden your perspective of programming by examining these languages side-by-side. You'll learn something new from each, and best of all, you'll learn how to learn a language quickly.

Bruce A. Tate
(328 pages) ISBN: 9781934356593. $34.95
http://pragprog.com/titles/btlang

Testing is only the beginning

Start with Test Driven Development, Domain Driven Design, and Acceptance Test Driven Planning in Ruby. Then add Shoulda, Cucumber, Factory Girl, and Rcov for the ultimate in Ruby and Rails development.

Behaviour-Driven Development (BDD) gives you the best of Test Driven Development, Domain Driven Design, and Acceptance Test Driven Planning techniques, so you can create better software with self-documenting, executable tests that bring users and developers together with a common language.

Get the most out of BDD in Ruby with *The RSpec Book*, written by the lead developer of RSpec, David Chelimsky.

David Chelimsky, Dave Astels, Zach Dennis, Aslak Hellesøy, Bryan Helmkamp, Dan North
(448 pages) ISBN: 9781934356371. $38.95
http://pragprog.com/titles/achbd

Rails Test Prescriptions is a comprehensive guide to testing Rails applications, covering Test-Driven Development from both a theoretical perspective (why to test) and from a practical perspective (how to test effectively). It covers the core Rails testing tools and procedures for Rails 2 and Rails 3, and introduces popular add-ons, including RSpec, Shoulda, Cucumber, Factory Girl, and Rcov.

Noel Rappin
(368 pages) ISBN: 9781934356647. $34.95
http://pragprog.com/titles/nrtest

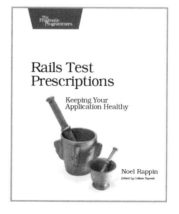

Welcome to the New Web

The world isn't quite ready for the new web standards, but you can be. Get started with HTML5, CSS3, and a better JavaScript today.

CoffeeScript is JavaScript done right. It provides all of JavaScript's functionality wrapped in a cleaner, more succinct syntax. In the first book on this exciting new language, CoffeeScript guru Trevor Burnham shows you how to hold onto all the power and flexibility of JavaScript while writing clearer, cleaner, and safer code.

Trevor Burnham
(160 pages) ISBN: 9781934356784. $29
http://pragprog.com/titles/tbcoffee

HTML5 and CSS3 are the future of web development, but you don't have to wait to start using them. Even though the specification is still in development, many modern browsers and mobile devices already support HTML5 and CSS3. This book gets you up to speed on the new HTML5 elements and CSS3 features you can use right now, and backwards compatible solutions ensure that you don't leave users of older browsers behind.

Brian P. Hogan
(280 pages) ISBN: 9781934356685. $33
http://pragprog.com/titles/bhh5

Advanced Ruby and Rails

What used to be the realm of experts is fast becoming the stuff of day-to-day development. Jump to the head of the class in Ruby and Rails.

Rails 3 is a huge step forward. You can now easily extend the framework, change its behavior, and replace whole components to bend it to your will, all without messy hacks. This pioneering book is the first resource that deep dives into the new Rails 3 APIs and shows you how to use them to write better web applications and make your day-to-day work with Rails more productive.

José Valim
(184 pages) ISBN: 9781934356739. $33
http://pragprog.com/titles/jvrails

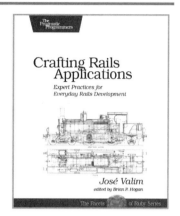

As a Ruby programmer, you already know how much fun it is. Now see how to unleash its power, digging under the surface and exploring the language's most advanced features: a collection of techniques and tricks known as *metaprogramming*. Once the domain of expert Rubyists, metaprogramming is now accessible to programmers of all levels—from beginner to expert. *Metaprogramming Ruby* explains metaprogramming concepts in a down-to-earth style and arms you with a practical toolbox that will help you write great Ruby code.

Paolo Perrotta
(296 pages) ISBN: 9781934356470. $32.95
http://pragprog.com/titles/ppmetr

The Pragmatic Bookshelf

The Pragmatic Bookshelf features books written by developers for developers. The titles continue the well-known Pragmatic Programmer style and continue to garner awards and rave reviews. As development gets more and more difficult, the Pragmatic Programmers will be there with more titles and products to help you stay on top of your game.

Visit Us Online

This Book's Home Page
http://pragprog.com/titles/jkdepj
Source code from this book, errata, and other resources. Come give us feedback, too!

Register for Updates
http://pragprog.com/updates
Be notified when updates and new books become available.

Join the Community
http://pragprog.com/community
Read our weblogs, join our online discussions, participate in our mailing list, interact with our wiki, and benefit from the experience of other Pragmatic Programmers.

New and Noteworthy
http://pragprog.com/news
Check out the latest pragmatic developments, new titles and other offerings.

Save on the eBook

Save on the eBook versions of this title. Owning the paper version of this book entitles you to purchase the electronic versions at a terrific discount.

PDFs are great for carrying around on your laptop—they are hyperlinked, have color, and are fully searchable. Most titles are also available for the iPhone and iPod touch, Amazon Kindle, and other popular e-book readers.

Buy now at *http://pragprog.com/coupon*

Contact Us

Online Orders:	*http://pragprog.com/catalog*
Customer Service:	*support@pragprog.com*
International Rights:	*translations@pragprog.com*
Academic Use:	*academic@pragprog.com*
Write for Us:	*http://pragprog.com/write-for-us*
Or Call:	+1 800-699-7764